To Karen,
You make
better place by just
being in it!
Wishing you the best
now and always!

Kia Piott 1/9/22

The
RELATIONSHIP

Animal Stories,
Human Insights:
A Guide to Improved Relationships

STEPHEN T. SCOTT

Teresa Granberry/Harvest Creek Publishing & Design
12050 White Oak Ranch Drive
Conroe, Texas 77304
www.harvestcreek.net

Cover and Book Layout © 2021 Harvest Creek Design
Chapter Imagery by Dawna Hacera

Ordering Information:
Quantity sales discounts are available by corporations, associations, and others. For details, please contact info@thehoustonbusinesscoach.com

The Relationship Zoo/Stephen T. Scott. —1ˢᵗ ed.

ISBN 978-1-7373567-2-1 Trade paperback
Printed in the United States of America

This book is dedicated to:

T-Tender, L-Loving, C-Care

These three words are the foundation for happier and more fulfilling relationships. These words speak the universal language that every human being, regardless of their origin, understands. That language is Kindness.

Kindness, along with the courtesy and consideration they bring, never goes out of style. It is timeless.

With more **T**ender, **L**oving, **C**are in your relationships, you will discover more opportunities for happiness and fulfillment.

TABLE OF CONTENTS

INTRODUCTION

WHAT IS A ZOO? A zoo is many things, but two ideas come to mind as it pertains to relationships. First, **a zoo has indoor and outdoor settings where living animals are kept and observed.** When we visit a zoo, it can be entertaining, and we can learn a great deal about the animals and their behavior.

Secondly, **a zoo can be a situation marked by confusion.** When looking at human relationships, whether indoors or outdoors, we observe and learn from our behaviors and others'. These can be good entertainment and fun. Or they can be draining, unhappy and confusing.

There is no definitive book that covers everything and all situations one may encounter in relationships. If there was, all of us would have read it and followed its teachings, to then live happily ever after.

Relationships are an art form. Each one of us puts our brush strokes on the canvas that is our relationships. Like a zoo where no two animals are exactly the same, each of us has a unique way of creating and approaching our relationships.

In reading *The Relationship Zoo: Animal Stories, Human Insights: A Guide to Improved Relationships,* I hope you will discover new perspectives and ways of thinking. And that you can apply them immediately to create pathways to improved and happier relationships.

Know that improvement only begins when you change your thinking. By changing your thoughts, you will change how you habitually conduct yourself in your relationships. Changes to your thinking and conduct ultimately change your results.

How should you read this book? Except for two of them, each chapter starts with a story about animals and their relationships with direct human parallels when carefully observed. These stories are followed by a series of short observations, thoughts, and truths on relationships to guide you on the adventure of life in *your* relationship zoo. These are not necessarily related to the story at the beginning of the chapter but instead are there to guide you on the adventure of life in *your* relationship zoo.

Once again, **the goal is to get you to think about your behavior and attitudes and, where applicable, to take action to move your relationships forward.**

I suggest that the best way to read this book is to **open it daily**. After all, if the book is never opened, you will not receive any benefit. Instead, turn to any page and begin reading. Then, if you prefer, skip around. Find something that captures your imagination. **Have fun!** The order in which you read the material is not essential.

The most important thing is that **the book is open. So now your mind will be available** to many things you can do to take your relationships to a happier and more fulfilling level.

Thank you for your time and attention in reading this book. I hope you discover things that will be positive, leading to **more peace and happiness in your relationships.**

All the best!

Steve Scott, Author

CHAPTER 1

Ants and Relationships

WHEN IT COMES TO RELATIONSHIPS, people should study ants. Ants have an amazing philosophy that applies to relationships. After all, ants need the connection to and support of other ants to survive. You will not see an ant straying off from the colony and living by itself. It would not survive because it understands that to live, it needs the other ants. So, what can we learn from them that can support us in *our* relationships?

Ants are persistent; they never quit. If an ant encounters an obstacle, it will find another way to overcome it. Great relationships are built on persistence in overcoming the inevitable obstacles. If you do not overcome, then the quality of your relationships will deteriorate.

Ants understand there are seasons—the two most important being summer and winter. For people, summer in a relationship pertains to the good times. Always take advantage of the summertime by stocking up on good memories. It is vital to have an inventory of these to remind you of your ability to produce good times.

Ants also know that there is winter. When it gets cold, ants realize it is time to rest and prepare for spring and summer. In your relationships, there will be times when things cool off. That is your time to reflect and to evaluate yourself and your relationships. Understanding that there will be winter is a critical perspective. You cannot be so naive in your relationships that you think summer and the good times will last forever. But, again, the good memories and experiences of summer get you through the challenging times of winter and create pathways to better experiences that will come when the following summer arrives.

Finally, ants always do all they possibly can. You do not see them taking time off. They understand that life is a limited-time offer, and they need to take advantage of it while they can. In your relationships, bring an attitude that you will do all you possibly can. Go "all-in" with relationships that truly matter. This does not guarantee success, but it will put the odds in your favor. Only when you give it all you can, do you have the possibility of genuinely great relationships.

In your relationships, learn from the ants. Be persistent. Understand that there will be seasons. Act accordingly. And always give all that you possibly can!

Additional Observations from
The Relationship Zoo

What Restores Reason?

Everyone uses reasoning abilities to justify their thoughts and actions. We use reasoning in many areas as well as to solve problems and to embrace opportunities. However, in relationships, when we offer our reason(s) for doing something and the other party questions or disagrees with our logic, things can become very heated. In defense of our reasoning, we often respond to the other person with even more logic or reasons why we are "right." But this accomplishes only one thing—it heightens the tension and anger. What can you do about this?

We think that somehow if we can outreason the other person, they will admit defeat and go along with us. But unfortunately, it does not work that way. So, when things get heated and you are trying to restore reason, remember this: Love restores reason and not the other way around.

Show the other person love by genuinely trying to understand what is at the root of their objections to your reasons. By doing this, you demonstrate that you value them.

Does this always work? Of course not! But, if you understand that love restores reason and not the other way around, you will have fewer bad arguments which rob you of energy, focus, and happiness. And you will increase the odds of sustaining positive relationships.

Apologizing

Changed behavior is the best apology. Why? Because changed behavior, which is lasting and sincere, shows that you have profoundly changed your thinking. And you now understand where you can genuinely improve in caring about and valuing others. Changed behavior emphasizes "we" instead of "me," building improved relationships while you become a better person in the process. Apologize with changed behavior because your actions will always speak louder than your words.

Arrogance

A significant error that is made in relationships is that people refuse to be humbled by their mistakes. And, immediately, they do the worst thing. They cover it up with arrogance. They will tell others, "It's not that big a deal." "You have done worse." Or, since they are uncomfortable acknowledging their mistake, they will talk about some unrelated achievement that in their mind positions them to where you are supposed to accept their reasoning and overlook their mistake.

Humility makes you more authentic and trustworthy to others. Arrogance distances you from others because you are trying to cover up your inadequacies and low self-esteem. Arrogance is never the foundation for healthy relationships.

The Eraser

Look at the eraser on a pencil. It is small and gets smaller when used after each mistake. Breaking trust in a relationship is a mistake that no eraser can completely erase, no matter how large.

How Do You See It?

The world can change in an instant. But can you change in an instant the way you choose to see it, and more importantly, yourself? The answer for most of us is no. When confronted with change, are you choosing to see it through the filter of the negative? Are you having trouble finding the good and the positive in yourself, let alone others? Most of us have had this challenge at one time or another. For better relationships in trying times, first see the good in yourself. Then it is much easier to see the good in others. Find the good. Be the good. And you will receive the good.

An Eye for an Eye

To have better relationships with those people who truly matter to you, you must give up the idea of paybacks and focus on givebacks. An eye for an eye, which is about paybacks or retribution, leaves everyone blind. Also, it causes you to focus on anger and animosity, which never make you a better person.

Don't become blind to the opportunity to be better and to give back to others. When you are blind to giving back, better opportunities in your relationships and life will become blind to finding you.

Being Deeply Loved

Lao Tzu said, "*Being deeply loved by someone gives you strength, while loving someone deeply gives you courage.*" Being loved by someone gives you strength in their acceptance and approval of you as a person. Loving someone takes courage because you are vulnerable to being hurt. Even though you love another person who is not perfect, you are tested daily to love them as well as one other imperfect person like them, perfectly. Who is the other person? It is you. Only when you love yourself first can you truly give love to others.

How Ships Sink

Here is an interesting fact: A ship never sinks because of the water around it. It only sinks because of the water that gets in it. So, one of the keys to your personal buoyancy and staying afloat is not to let what is happening around you weigh you down on the inside and cause you to sink.

To keep the ship that is your life afloat and headed on course, always have mechanisms for coping with and bailing out the negative thoughts and emotions that could sink you. How? Focus on your positive vision of the future.

Have your future destination finished in your mind. Once the future is finished in your mind, then what you need to do in the present to keep from sinking and stay on course to better, safer harbors become crystal clear. With a well-defined picture of a successful future destination, you will be better prepared to keep your ship afloat when the storms of life come your way.

A Merry Heart

Proverbs 17:22 says, "*A merry heart doeth good like a medicine: but a broken spirit drieth the bones.*" There is a happiness advantage that comes with a merry heart. Studies have shown that there are many positive outcomes when you are happy. You will accomplish more, enjoy life more, and have better relationships, to name a few. Focus on what you are thankful for. Do it daily. Make it a habit. When you do, you will create your own happiness advantage in relationships and life.

Toxic People

The only way to win with a toxic person in the playground of life is to leave the playground. A toxic person must have someone to play with to succeed. Many people think that by leaving the playground of a toxic person, they have suffered a defeat. Reality says that by staying, you will constantly be drained and feel defeated.

Victory comes in knowing where to place your relationships. It comes when you understand that there are three things you can do with any relationship. You can either expand it, limit it, or delete it. In many cases hitting the delete button is the hardest. But with a toxic person, it is necessary to delete them if you will move forward with your life.

Fall and Rise

All of us fall. The key to success is to rise every time you fall. Every time you fail, whether in business, life, or relationships, it takes you down into the valley. Being in the valley becomes an opportunity to rise and scale a new peak in the mountain range of life. How do you do this? First, get a vision of what you want your success to look like. Then, with a clear vision, you have created your own internal GPS to climb to new peaks to view success and realize better relationships.

Choose Your Friends Wisely

Choose your friends wisely. The power and influence of our associations are far-reaching. What do the people in your life have you thinking about? What do they have you watching? What do they have you reading? All of these are important. The influence of your friends is the perspective you will bring into any new relationship. Is that perspective positive or negative? Choose your friends wisely!

Relationship Scars

All of us have scars from relationships that were hurtful or hateful (the list could go on and on). The bottom line is that they did not work out. The question is: Have you formed scar tissue from these experiences? Scar tissue means that healing has taken place. Scar tissue is stronger than regular tissue. With scar tissue, you are now ready to move on to better relationships.

Yet, if you keep revisiting the past, then scar tissue never forms. The wound is always open. And you will attract those who are good at working on the wound because that is where you have decided to focus. But, at the same time, they are not good at helping you heal and moving you beyond it. So, ultimately, this is not a foundation for good relationships.

Develop your relationship scars. Get healed. Only when you are healed are you ready for better relationships.

Pessimism

Pessimism is a jail for the human spirit. When in jail, you cannot discover new things, develop new skills, and most importantly, you cannot serve others with a positive benefit. Also, pessimism and its focus on the negative will take the ship that is your life and sail it into the rocks to sink. Focus on the positive, where you want your ship to sail. Adjust your course along the way. Deal with the negative, as positive people do, as a learning experience to guide your life to better and safer harbors.

Lasting Relationships

For successful relationships that last, you must come together, keep together, and work together. Coming together is what begins a relationship. Keeping together, despite obstacles, is a must if you are to work together. Whether with one individual or many, working together takes the connection to the highest level, a performing team. And you must have one other key ingredient, similar values. Only with similar values can you realize the benefits that come from long-term successful relationships.

Fire, Sparks, Success, Happiness

There are times when our fire just about goes out. Yet, another human being shows up and blows the dying embers into a flame. Be sure to show appreciation and gratitude to those who have rekindled your fire. Very often, they saw something in you that you did not.

Life is a contact sport. Only through contact are there sparks with others who can light your flame. So, for a more successful and happier life, not to mention better relationships, seek out those who provide the sparks that will ignite or enlarge your flame.

The Words You Speak

The house you live in is the words you speak to others. The words you speak are a manifestation of your self-talk, what is going on inside of you. What are you saying when you talk to yourself? Are you grateful? Are you angry? Are you resentful? Are you happy?

There are many more. The words you speak reflect the house in which you live. And they will determine the people you invite into your life and the quality of your relationships.

What Are You Projecting?

Noted philosopher Marcus Aurelius once said, *"Very little is needed to make a happy life; it is all within yourself in your way of thinking."* Thoughts are things. Be grateful in your thoughts about your life and your relationships. What you project on others will come back to you. What are you projecting? Show and give others gratitude and happiness, and you will attract more people who are grateful and happy. These are key steps to a happier life.

To Be Somebody

All of us need to feel valued. Unfortunately, in trying to be somebody, many people make the mistake of trying to be" interesting" to others. When you realize you are trying to be "interesting," stop. Put your focus first on others. Be interested in them. Being interested in others is the only way to add value to others while allowing you to connect more deeply. To be somebody to others be interested in them.

Wrapped Up in Yourself

Being wrapped up in yourself makes for a ridiculously small package. "We" is always larger than "me." There is tremendous power in the word: Let's. For example, "Let us (i.e., we) build something together." What a contrast this statement is from "Let me do it by myself."

Alone I (i.e., me) can accomplish some things. But together, we (you and I) can blend our talents. You can do what I cannot do, and I can do what you cannot. When we join together, we can accomplish great things. That is the power of relationships.

You Can Never Be Great If ...

It is hard to be great if you don't choose your friends wisely. It is hard to be great if you don't let go of your need to be correct. It is hard to be great if you are always offended. It is hard to be great when you are upset with yourself and think less of yourself.

It is hard to be great if the words you speak lessen the value of others. It is hard to be great if you are full of hatred, anger, and depression. It is hard to be great if you cannot love people to where you understand them.

You can still have some degree of greatness with the above items. All of us have them or have experienced them. It is a matter of managing the areas where we need improvement. As someone once said, we have two characteristics: we are awesome, and we are awful.

To the point of being awesome, to being great, you can never be great with a grudge. A grudge will control you. So, you must learn how to forgive others. You must learn how to let go.

And, most importantly, you must forgive yourself. When you have a grudge against yourself, you can never be great. Forgive yourself. Forgiving yourself frees you from you. And with forgiveness, you have opened the pathways to be all that you can be, to better relationships, and to be great.

You Have a Choice Every Day

You have a choice every day. Are you choosing to be grateful? Are you choosing to be happy? Are you choosing to be enthusiastic? Our thoughts are things that have emotions attached to them. They are the things that manifest themselves in our daily lives and, more importantly, our relationships. Your life will reflect your choices of thought, which is empowering! Your life will be as you wish!

> *Your life will reflect your choices of thought, which is empowering!*

Worry

All of us have some worry. Yet, when we become preoccupied with worry, it is like praying for what we do not want. So instead, intentionally keep your mind on what you want. Focus on what brings you peace.

When you do, people will feel safe around you. However, when you are always expressing your worries, it will drive people away from you. Worry brings uncertainty, and uncertainty very often leads to a lack of trust. That is not an atmosphere that others feel comfortable in, let alone for having good relationships.

Without trust, it is not possible to have healthy relationships. Worry is a part of life, yet it does not have to be your life. Focus on what you can control, not what you cannot. That will position you to move forward to creating and having the relationships and life you desire.

KEY TAKEAWAYS:

✓ Ants demonstrate many positive qualities in relationships, including persistence, determination, and reliance on teamwork.

✓ It is acceptable to remove yourself from toxic relationships.

✓ Your thoughts guide the outcome of your life.

✓ Create a vision of what you want your life to be; it will serve as a GPS to guide you.

✓ Make a choice every day to harness your thoughts for something positive.

CHAPTER 2

Hand Closed, Hand Open

IN AFRICA, they have a unique way of capturing monkeys. Unfortunately, monkeys can be very disruptive and destructive as their curiosity gets them into many things. These wary little animals are very fond of rice. So, to capture them, local farmers put some rice inside a hollow coconut shell, into which they have cut a hole just large enough for the monkey's hand. Half a dozen traps like this are left lying around in the center of the village. But each one is attached by a string to a nearby hut.

A family of monkeys comes up, attracted by the smell of the rice. Each slips its hand into a shell to get a handful of rice. But with its hand full, it is unable to remove it. The hunters then approach and easily gather their prey. If the monkey would only let go of the rice, it would be able to get away from the trap set for it. But it likes rice too much to give it up—even at the risk of its life.

Suppose we approach relationships like the monkeys, grabbing onto something for our sustenance and never letting go. We will lose or kill the good in the relationship. A hand that is closed while holding something is never in a position to give. Having the palm open with the hand facing up puts you in a position to give as well as to receive. Knowing how to give and to receive is essential to creating possibilities for good relationships.

Additional Observations from
The Relationship Zoo

What Gives Up First

When faced with obstacles, especially physical ones, the mind will give up before the body. That is also true in our quest for success and fulfillment. The mind will give up on our desire to grow and to add value to ourselves. To keep going and growing, you must buy into the idea of sowing and reaping. In and of itself, this action encourages you to continue because you expect something good from your efforts.

The same is true in your relationships. Keep sowing and reaping. In your relationships as well as life, sowing and reaping are a sorting process. Not all crops or relationships that you reap are going to be good. When they are not, look at what you were sowing. Was it anger? Was it a sense of inadequacy? Was it an unmet or unstated expectation? There are many more.

Keep your mind focused on sowing and reaping to move forward in your relationships and life; that is only accomplished through purposeful action. If you watch the wind, you will not sow. If you watch the clouds, you will not reap. Success and the resulting growth and fulfillment it brings into your relationships and life comes when you don't give up in your mind.

Finding Someone Wonderful

Most of us have sought to find someone wonderful to complement our lives. I have done that, and I am sure many of you have done that, as well. But, at a low time in your life, when you are searching for someone wonderful to step into it, change it, and lift you up, consider this: The person that could lift you up is with you right now—it is you!

It is you when you decide to be inner-directed. And, regardless of people, circumstances, or things, you choose to tap into this power of being inner-directed. To see the change you desire, you must first be the change. Be the change, and you will have found someone wonderful. You will also be pleased with the opportunities and the relationships that will be attracted into your life.

Dirty Feet

The quality of your life and your level of happiness is determined by the character of the people you most associate with. Do you feel better or worse after you have been with someone? Those with dirty feet walk through your heart, your mind and leave a mess. Expand those relationships with people who don't have dirty feet for a more fulfilling and happier life. Limit those who at times may or may not leave a muddy footprint. And delete those who leave dirty footprints all the time. They are not suitable for you. Know what your relationships are doing to you. Avoid the ones with dirty feet!

Know what your relationships are doing to you. Avoid the ones with dirty feet!

The Power of the Tongue

Two significant components of any successful relationship are the words we use and the tone with which they are delivered. For better relationships, focus on what you have to be grateful for. Express this gratitude in your words. Have positive intentionality. Be positive on purpose.

This does not mean that you put on rose-colored glasses to not see the negative for what it is. It just means that you don't put your focus on it. Instead, look for the good things to talk about to bring peace and even prosperity to a relationship. There is life and death in the power of your tongue.

The Bible teaches that Samson slew one-thousand Philistines with the jawbone of an ass. Yet, I have seen that weapon used every day on ourselves. Don't get hung by your tongue. Have positive intentionality. Respect the power of your tongue.

Difficult Times

A difficult time can be more readily met and lived through if you have the firm belief that your life has meaning beyond the current circumstances. Always keep your vision of the future you desire in mind. What is your purpose in life? Do you have a cause that you support? Are there goals you wish to achieve? Who are the people that love you, and you love them?

Purpose, along with your sense of being and a strong belief in yourself, will give you the perspective to endure challenging times. Purpose is the necessary fuel to overcome difficulties. And good relationships will give that fuel the octane boost and support that will drive you to prevail over the obstacles and get back on the road to success and happiness.

Inside-Out

Your relationship with yourself is your primary and most powerful relationship. Everything starts from within and manifests itself on the outside. Your thoughts, words, and actions concerning how you feel about yourself are what you project on others. What are you projecting? What is that bringing to your relationships?

The Fuel That Drives Love

Trust is the fuel that drives love. Without trust, love comes to a stop.

Courage and Accomplishment

Courage has several angles to it. First, it may be doing something that scares you. Second, it could be demonstrating strength in the face of pain or grief or showing bravery in a challenging situation.

In your life, courage is a necessary component for success. Courage says that you will take the risk to learn from your mistakes. And, in applying what you know, you will not be defeated. You will try again. Courage says, even when things are discouraging that you will see them through to the end.

Courage says that you care enough about yourself and others to give your best even if you are not assured of a desirable outcome. Have and show the courage to overcome. Your life will not be measured as much by what you accomplish as it will be by your courage and what you have had to overcome to accomplish.

Here is another benefit of courage: It will open up opportunities for positive relationships because your authenticity will attract people. Show others your courage, and you will attract the people who truly get you and appreciate you for who you are.

Arguments

Arguments. They happen. The causes are infinite. And usually, relationships are hurt, not helped. Why? In an argument, there is always a winner.

Conversely, there is also always a loser. Arguments are win-lose propositions that can weaken the best of relationships. If you see yourself heading down the argument path, remember that discussions are always better than arguments.

But once the anger is ignited in an argument, the focus becomes on *who* is right rather than on *what* is right. Understanding others is where the real miracles of good relationships are born, nurtured, and deepened.

When You Are Upset with Yourself

Your self-talk has a powerful influence on you and your relationships with others. All of us make mistakes and get upset with ourselves. When that happens, there is something you can do to make things better.

When you are upset with yourself, don't think any less of yourself, but instead think of yourself less. How do you go about doing that? Give something good to others, such as a phone call, a personal visit, or an email or text. Or serve others, which is the quickest way to take your mind off of yourself.

Also, when you are out doing good, it is much easier to forgive yourself and move forward. So, the next time you are upset with yourself, don't think less of yourself. Think of yourself less.

Hard Knocks and Soft Touches

In our relationships, there are times when we either give or receive hard knocks or soft touches. The hard knocks and the soft touches each convey different emotions. Bring the full spectrum of emotions to your relationships. If you don't, it is like bringing a splinter from a log instead of the whole log to start a fire. Like the splinter of wood, revealing a small part of yourself may get some sparks, but it won't sustain the fire. Bring your emotions, the hard knocks, and the soft touches, and people will know better how to connect with you positively. Why? Because you have created more avenues for authentic connection.

Teams

When two individuals come together in a relationship, they form a team. How well that team performs depends on the individual members. What can be forgotten is that the strength of each member in a relationship is the team. On the teams in your life, realize that you cannot be you, "me" without "we." And that "we" cannot be what it is without "me." Together the whole is much greater than the sum of the parts.

Count to Turn Your Life Around

To turn your life around, begin counting by the numbers. Start counting your blessings every day. Your gratitude will bring a change in attitude that will turn your life around. You are blessed with talents and abilities. Yet, your attitude will determine how much and how well you get to use them.

Be grateful. Put yourself in a position to use your gifts and talents. In turn, not only will you be happier, but you will be giving the gift of happiness to others.

Ultimately, those who are not grateful do not find happiness attracted to them. Count your blessings. Happiness is attracted to those who are grateful. And, without happiness, there is no true success.

Getting Even

"Getting even" is the belief that you can right some injustice, slight or hurt, by seeing the person who you believed caused this to be hurt themselves. Here is the truth: Trying to get even with those who have wronged you is a natural reaction. Your anger is valid. Yet, it keeps you focused on the negative in your life. And, when you carry anger or have not put it in a safe place, it is toxic to you, your energy, your performance, and your relationships. If you let it, it will occupy rent-free space in your mind and your heart.

The next time you are hurt, don't seek to lash back. That only keeps you focused on the negative. Instead, turn it into a positive. How? Invest your time and energy in getting even with those who believe in you, support you and bless you. Believe in them, support them, and most importantly, bless them. Then, focus on doing good which will put you in a positive mood. And a positive attitude increases the odds of attracting more of what the good life has to offer. So, to move forward, get even by doing good.

Be the Change! Remain Relevant!

Socrates taught that "*The secret of change is to focus all of your energy, not on fighting the old, but on building the new.*" Embracing change is the first step in building something new. Yet, to be successful in building the new, whether in your business, relationships, or life, it starts with you. You must be relevant; otherwise, you will not connect with others. If you are irrelevant, others will not connect with you. Be the change. Be relevant. Connect with others!

Sparks

You are alive! You have sparks of life inside of you. Where these sparks are most appreciated is when you share them with others. Something you do or say can spark someone to do or accomplish things they did not think were possible. Not only are they better, but you feel better about yourself and the positives you have created. But there are times when

Give to others what you want, that spark of life.

you don't feel or have the spark. When this occurs, force yourself to go and give positive energy, a spark to others. Give to others what you want, that spark of life. You are much more likely to receive their spark of life and energy in return when you do.

Dogs and Relationships

All of us do foolish things at times. With my dog, I can behave foolishly or say something stupid, and she looks at me with a look that says, "Wow, you are entertaining. What's up?" Or, if I say nonsense to her, she gives me a look that says, "Wow, you are brilliant! I would never have thought to say it that way!" The best part about a dog, unlike human relationships, is your foolishness will never be revealed. With people, it is a different story. They will dog you about your folly.

Color Outside the Lines

When you keep the same boundaries in your life, it becomes like a picture that never changes. No matter how you color it inside the edges or lines, an unchanging image can become the zone of mediocrity. Only when you change the picture of your comfort zone and color outside your current limits and lines will you and your life change. As you color outside the lines, you will encounter new people. You will develop new relationships creating unforeseen possibilities for growth and fulfillment.

One

One seed can start a tree. One tree can provide life-sustaining shade. One act of kindness can begin a friendship. One act of service can lift others. One word of encouragement can spur significant accomplishments. One laugh and one candle can turn dark on the inside and outside into light. One soft touch can radiate a sense of well-being.

And one life—your life—can be the positive tipping point in someone's day. Be that one! It all starts with you. Be that one who makes a positive difference.

Bad Mood and Bad Words

When you are in a bad mood, what are the words that you speak? Your mood can change, but the words you speak can never be replaced. The words you speak today are heard by the ears attached to the mouth that will repeat them tomorrow.

What stories do you want others to be telling about you? It is much easier to forgive or overlook someone's bad mood, let alone forget about it when harsh words don't get in the way. For better relationships, be careful of the words you choose.

Your Life is Your Cause

"I would rather fail in a cause that will ultimately triumph than triumph in a cause that will ultimately fail." (President Woodrow Wilson). Your life is your cause. What you share and give to others is how they will see you and your life regardless of obstacles and setbacks. So, live a life of sharing and giving to others while taking care of yourself. When you do, the cause of your life, and the relationships that reflect it, will leave a legacy of triumph.

 **KEY TAKEAWAYS**

✓ Winning an argument or being "right" isn't always a victory.

✓ Moods and attitudes impact the words that you speak.

✓ Courage is often more impressive than accomplishment.

✓ Understand the power of one.

✓ Legacies are created through your life's cause. Find your life's purpose by first believing in yourself.

CHAPTER 3

What Are You Seeing?

IN THE FOLLOWING STORY, nature shows us the importance of movement and how to obtain more. In nature, the currency isn't money; it is food. Therefore, food in nature is the equivalent of cash. And, in nature, you must have the proper movement to acquire food successfully.

The Portia Spider is unique in nature. It is the only spider that exists with the mission to kill and eat other spiders. The Portia spider lives and eats through carefully choreographed movement. There is no wasted motion. It disguises itself as a leaf or twig as it moves onto another spider's web. Thus, it does not arouse any suspicion.

Remember that spiders have extremely poor vision. So, when the web traps an insect, the host spider with impaired vision comes out to eat it. At this time, the unsuspecting spider is attacked by the Portia spider, making a meal of it. That's one way it accomplishes its mission to get fed.

In our relationships, we want to get fed. In the heat of the moment, we can lose our vision. And when we do, it can be hurtful and costly. But the story of the Portia spider does not end here.

The Portia spider also does something even more subtle. And this subtlety in its movement is the key to its success. It has another way, even more clever, to attract its victims. It will sit in another spider's web and, for up to 3 days, simulate the harmonic motion in the web of a captured insect. It is always trying to lure the host spider to come and check out the prey that it can feel and hear but cannot see. The Portia spider has good vision for a spider. When the host spider comes to check what is caught in the web, in one quick motion the Portia spider attacks the host spider, kills it, and eats it.

How does this apply to your relationships? First, don't get caught in the wrong web. When first getting to know someone, carefully note how they talk, act, and, most importantly, treat others. You can't see everything.

Always check your feelings. If it doesn't feel right, you very well may be entering a web that will be toxic to the relationship. Like the spiders that are victims of the Portia spider, poor vision can lead to unhappiness even if things seem or feel right.

Additional Observations from The Relationship Zoo

Hatred, Anger, and Depression

I had a conversation with a psychiatrist about hatred, anger, and depression. Of course, we discussed other mental and psychological challenges, but what struck me was that hatred, anger, and depression are often a failure of imagination—a failure to imagine a better outcome, a better world, better relationships.

Also, very often, our imaginations fail to create a better picture. Consequently, we act our way into making the negative we imagine a reality because we have little faith in ourselves. When we have little faith, at least hatred, anger and depression fill us with something and give us some feelings. There are many hatred, anger, and depression cases where imagination is not a step, let alone a cure. But as a normal human being, it is natural to experience all three of these at times. But, to get stuck and overwhelmed because of them is frightening. They can paralyze us.

The next time you encounter these feelings, try using your imagination to create a better scenario. Create a vision of the future you desire. Then, stay with it every day. The only way we overcome anything is one day at a time. And, when you overcome yourself, you are on your way to better relationships and a fuller life.

How To Change Your Relationships

Rumi, the great Persian poet, once said, *"Yesterday I was clever, so I wanted to change the world. Today I am wise, so I am changing myself."* Do you want your relationships to change? To be better? To be more fulfilling? Change yourself, and you will change the world, and how the world sees you will change, too.

Choices

You have the power within you to make choices every single day. And those choices will determine how you feel about yourself, your day, and your life. For example, you can choose to be grateful. You can choose to be appreciative or choose to complain. You can choose to be happy, or you can choose to be angry. You can choose to feel blessed or decide to be troubled. The list of choices goes on and on.

Negative things, unexpectedly, will happen to all of us and knock us off

Your life will reflect your choices of thought. course at times. Yet, we still have the power of choice. So, the next time life throws you a curve or knocks you off track, choose to find a way to get back on course. It may take some time. But do make that choice to pick yourself up and move forward.

As my mother would tell me as I was growing up, you must develop coping skills. Choose thoughts to move you and your life forward. Thoughts are things. Your life will reflect your choices of thought. This is empowering. Your life will be as you wish!

Gratitude

Counting your blessings daily, in a purposeful way, will turn your life around. It will lead to improved relationships. Gratitude allows you to focus on what you have and to be grateful for it. Ungrateful people do not find happiness attracted to them. Happiness is attracted to those who are grateful. Be thankful, and you will attract and discover happiness. Without happiness, there is no true success.

Hurt

Hurt, at some point in time, in almost any relationship is inevitable. And to think that a few words can heal the hurt is unrealistic. When we are hurt, the best we can do is start a process to allow ourselves to feel better.

When we stand back from the hurt, most of us are not hurt as much by what happens to us as we are by our opinion of it. Unfortunately, our views of what happened are what hurts us most. To begin the process of moving beyond the hurt, look at it as a challenge to grow. Ask yourself how to use this hurt to become a better person. No, it wasn't your fault. But you must put hurt in a safe place where it does not infect your other relationships.

Only when you choose to grow from the hurt will you know how to handle it and, more importantly, feel good about yourself because you are putting it in a safe place. Also, this helps you be prepared if and when it shows up again.

Blame

A Chinese proverb reads, *"He who blames others has a long way to go on his journey. He who blames himself is halfway there. He who blames no one has arrived."* You are the captain of your life. You are responsible for it. Blaming people, circumstances, and things for negative results may be factually correct. Regardless, blame keeps you in the past as a victim. Blame and continually revisiting it is like pouring acid on all your relationships. It will eat away at some and burn others. People will distance themselves from acidity. You cannot change the past. But, if you choose to take responsibility for the present and move on from the past, you can create a *present* with relationships that will lead you to a better *future*.

Perseverance-The Relationship Filter

As you go through each day, you run a series of short races. That is really what the long race is, a series of short races day in and day out that hopefully take you where you want to go. Perseverance is a mindset. And when people see your perseverance to a goal, a dream, or living your life by design, they either find it energizing or threatening. Persevering daily will act as an excellent filter for which relationships you need to invest in and those where it is time to move on.

The Crowd

The crowd is the circle of relationships closest to you. The crowd communicates with you, has access to you, and influences you. Depending on who is in your crowd, it can keep you on course or distract you into areas that diminish your ability to accomplish.

If you feel your crowd is pushing you in the wrong direction, then it is time for you to walk alone. Going with the crowd when you know it is going in the wrong direction always leads to an inevitable, downward plunge in your life. Walk alone, even if you are not sure of your direction. You can live with yourself when you don't follow the crowd and do what is right.

What Truly Matters

Over time you discover what truly matters. What really matters is the quality of your relationships. Unfortunately, when time shows you what matters, you can regret what you have missed. Use the experiences that time has granted you as a school to learn from, not as a club on yourself. The past is past. Start today to discern the difference between what you believe is truly important and what truly matters. You will start making better decisions with your time for your life and your relationships, and that is what truly matters.

The Prescription for Unhappiness

If you want to be unhappy, constantly compare yourself to others. Someone always has it better, easier, etc. That's their highlight reel. And you keep playing the video of all your behind-the-scenes struggles. The comparison is never favorable, nor does it enhance your relationships. When you bring a diminished feeling about yourself into a relationship, it will have a negative impact.

So, what do you do? First, create your own highlight reel featuring your accomplishments and all you have to be grateful for. Next, go to work on yourself. Today, ask yourself, "Who is the person I want to become?" Only when you enlarge yourself and become more as a person, will you feel more secure, creating a highlight reel that brings positive energy to your relationships.

Bite Your Tongue or Eat Your Words?

Bite your tongue or eat your words is a choice all of us get to make in our relationships with others. I have observed that the more successful relationships in business and life are when people know when to bite their tongue. In these relationships, people have tact. Tact is a choice. Tact is an emotional safety valve to let you maneuver away from an uncomfortable situation without expending your mental and emotional capital.

Unfortunately, all of us make mistakes with words. Remember that when you have to eat your words, you will be constantly reminded of them in the future, whether in weeks, months, or years.

Self-Care

To have better relationships, you must be good at self-care. Self-care gives you the fuel that allows your light to shine brightly. How do you care for yourself? Three of the many areas to look at for self-care are: mental, emotional, and physical. Who do you hang with? What do you read? What do you watch on TV? What do you eat? How do you exercise? Very few of us are good in all of these areas. Be good in as many as possible with your self-care.

In a good relationship, I must care for myself to be the best for you. And you must take care of yourself to be the best for me. It is our responsibility to take care of ourselves, not someone else's. With good self-care, you will provide the fuel for your light to shine brightly and better your life and the lives of others.

The Relational Elevator

Self-improvement is your personal elevator. As you rise to the top, you will have to let some people off. When you focus on self-improvement, you are always in transition. As you climb, you must let go of those relationships that no longer serve you and the new person you are becoming.

If you don't, you will feel stuck, which eventually robs you of energy and happiness. Look at your relationships. Ask yourself, "Who do they have me becoming?" And then ask yourself, "Is this acceptable?"

If the answer is no, let that person off your relational elevator so you may continue your self-improvement and rise to greater heights.

Forgiveness

Many times, forgiveness is not easy. It's tough to get to that place where you forgive. Relational hurts can last a lifetime. But, to have healthy relationships with others, you must be able to forgive. Even if the relationship is no longer around, your forgiveness keeps you from producing the acid of anger and hate that will infect your good relationships.

In reality, forgiveness is not so much for the other person as it is for you. So, forgive and get rid of your grievances. The greatest benefit to you in the miracle process of forgiveness is that it frees you from you!

Love Yourself

To love another for who they are, you must first love yourself for who you are. Of course, this does not mean that you, I, or anyone else has to be perfect. To love ourselves means that we must accept ourselves. Only when you accept yourself for who you are can you bring peace to others. It's hard to give love to others if you can't give love to yourself.

Here are a couple of thoughts that may help you get to where you want to be. First, self-awareness leads to self-acceptance. How does it do this? It shows you your vulnerabilities. When you are vulnerable, you become authentic to others. And with authenticity comes trust, which allows you to build the deepest, happiest, and most meaningful relationships. Only when you love yourself can you positively love others.

Sing Anyway

If you have one of those days, as all of us will, where your energy is low and your enthusiasm is down, put a song in your heart. How do you do this? Every day, even on the rough days, find things and people to be grateful for. Start with the small things. The challenging days are made better with gratitude because it positions you to put a song in your heart. As a result, your days are more positive, not only in what you have to do but, more importantly, because your song will position you for potentially more positive relationships.

Kindness

Kindness is the universal language of human relationships. You do not need an interpreter for Kindness. An ancient Chinese philosopher once said, *"Kindness in words creates confidence. Kindness in thinking creates profoundness. Kindness in giving creates love."* Show Kindness. Express Kindness. Kindness will elevate you as the giver and lift those who receive it. And, as a result, all the people in your life and you will be better for it.

The Pain of Someone Ending Their Relationship with You

When someone we value chooses to end their relationship with us, it causes pain. To start moving to a better place, remember: What you focus on in the present determines not only your current emotional state but affects your current and future relationships. Your pain is valid and legitimate. Yet, focusing on the pain keeps you in the past, in a position of weakness, and thinking like a victim.

Focusing on pain is a prescription for unhappiness—not only for you but for the people in your life. Instead, focus on what you have learned and, more importantly, what you will change in your thinking and perspective to minimize the odds of the same thing happening in the future. Stay fixated on the past, and your odds are high that you will repeat the pain of what you just experienced. Instead, focus on what you learned, and the odds are higher that you will create better future relationships. What goes on inside us will manifest itself on the outside; it will be the primary driver of your success in your relationships.

Good Values

Without good values, it is a challenge to recognize what is right regarding morals and ethics. It is a challenge to make the right decisions and to associate with the right people. When you have good values, you will have better relationships. You will recognize the *right* thing when according to others, it is wrong. And you'll know the *wrong* thing when according to others, it is right.

Relationships built on sound values will clarify right and wrong that you can get from no other source. Have your relationships based on sound values, and you will experience greater peace of mind and happiness.

Giver or Taker?

Are you a giver or taker in your relationships? The answer is that to have successful relationships, you must be both. Most people predominantly fall to either the giver or the taker side. Neither is good or bad. It is a matter of degree.

Most of the time, if you are a giver, you probably have challenges taking care of yourself and doing things that make you happy. If you are a taker, your challenge is that people see you as needy and wanting to control them. Whatever your tendency, be self-aware and control your propensity to go too far.

For example, as a giver, my tendency can be to go too far in caring for others or having a "go along to get along" attitude. This happens even if I don't like what I have to do or who I have to get along with. So, all I am doing is creating unhappiness through my choice. And, then I bring that unhappiness into my relationships.

Learn how to modify your tendencies. Be self-aware. If you are a giver, to have better relationships, constructively learn how to take. If you are a taker, learn how to be more of a giver. To be a giver means giving others, where possible, what they want, not what you *think* they want. As a taker, if you give others what you think they want, you are still taking because you have to be in control.

The giver and taker are art forms. They are a balancing act. We are not always going to get it right. Yet, as long as we are self-aware of our tendencies, we can modify our behavior and take ourselves on paths to better relationships.

Stoop to Stand Tall in Your Relationships

You will never stand taller than when you stoop to help someone in need. As little kids, it was always great when a taller adult stooped to help us. The greatest gift you can give another person is the encouragement and support to be all they can be. Whether you are a child or an adult, the gift of encouragement is always appreciated. Positivity in relationships is about standing tall and encouraging others to be what they *can* be instead of what they *cannot.*

 **KEY TAKEAWAYS**

✓ Comparing oneself to others only leads to unhappiness.

✓ Forgiveness isn't for the person who caused the pain. Forgiveness is for you!

✓ Be mindful of the people (or "crowd") that you run with; they determine the direction you are heading.

✓ When it comes to relationships, quality matters more than quantity.

✓ Whether you are a giver or a taker, learn to cultivate balance in your life.

CHAPTER 4

Empowerment, Butterflies, and People

A MAN FOUND a cocoon for a butterfly. A small opening appeared in the cocoon; he sat and watched the butterfly for several hours as it struggled to force its body through the tiny hole. Then it seemed to stop making any progress. It appeared stuck.

The man decided to help the butterfly, and with a pair of scissors, he cut open the cocoon. The butterfly then emerged easily. But something was strange. The butterfly had a swollen body and shriveled wings. The man watched, expecting it to take on its correct proportions. But nothing changed. The butterfly remained the same. It was never able to fly.

In his kindness and haste, the man did not realize the butterfly's struggle to get through the small opening of the cocoon was nature's way of preparing the butterfly to fly. Requiring the butterfly to struggle through the small hole forced fluid from its body into its wings. Only through this process would the butterfly's wings be ready to support its natural instinct to fly.

In your relationships, it is essential to empower others. When we empower others, we let them struggle, learn, and grow. Empowerment is not about fixing someone.

Empowerment is a process to let others build themselves with our love and support. When we cut it short and do not allow people to take ownership of their growth, we lower their self-esteem. In turn, they feel diminished in our relationship with them and start moving away instead of toward us.

Additional Observations from
The Relationship Zoo

Past, Present, and Future Relationships

Past relationships are those that you had at one time but are no longer part of your present. Present relationships are the people you deal with today and regularly. Yet, the most important relationships will be your future ones.

Always be looking to form new, positive relationships. These relationships will have you climb mountains and see vistas that are unimaginable today. But to see this beautiful future, you must let go of those relationships in the present that keep you from climbing to new summits. Also, you must not dwell on

The key to reaching new levels of success and happiness in life is to pack your backpack with the right supplies.

the past. Poor past and present relationships will keep you anchored and unable to move forward.

The key to reaching new levels of success and happiness in life is to pack your backpack with the right supplies. Include people with good attitudes, and ultimately people who will encourage you to climb to the future you desire.

Have a Good Relationship with Yourself

"The secret to living well and longer is to: eat half, walk double, laugh triple, and love without measure." (Tibetan Proverb) Eat what you need. Exercise. See the humor in yourself and life. And love without measure because you have gratitude for all the good and blessings in your life. When you do all of these, you will have a good relationship with yourself. You will find more inner peace and increase your odds of living well and longer.

Admiration

Every day tell someone something you admire about them. When you express genuine admiration to someone, they will see a window of kindness and have a sense of safety. Kindness and safety are two magnets that attract better relationships. So, admire something about someone today and tell them. Admiration unspoken is admiration that is never known.

Be Happy Over the Good Fortune of Others

When you are happy over the good fortune of others, you will maintain your sanity and your joy. On the other hand, comparing someone else's good fortune to your present circumstances is a formula for jealousy, envy, and unhappiness.

Appreciation of others' good fortune is a beautiful thing. It allows you to take the good that has happened in others' lives and have it become part of your own. The benefit of appreciation is that it blesses you with a positive mental and emotional outlook that will enhance your relationships and your life.

You've Got One Time

Relationships are like restaurants. When you visit a restaurant, it has one opportunity to create a good experience. So likewise, every time you encounter someone, whether in person, by phone, video, text, or email, it is like visiting a restaurant—you have that one time to make it count.

Relationships are the summation of many small encounters. Look at each encounter as the one chance you have with your words and behavior to give your best and make the time count. After that, what the other person does is up to them.

No one likes a casual approach day in and day out. Why? Casualness leads to a lack of clarity. Lack of clarity leads to poor communication. But most importantly, casualness leads others to feel like they are being taken for granted. To have relationships with better clarity always place a high value on every interaction. You've got one time.

A Lesson from the Arrow

In archery, to shoot an arrow, you must first pull it backward. When difficulties and obstacles are confronting you, or even pulling you back, remember the arrow. Pulling back in your life is necessary to launch forward to hit new and better targets.

When in the valley of difficulty, get a firm picture of the life you desire. How are you going to add value to yourself? How are you going to serve others? Only with a target, which is your picture of the future, can you shoot the arrow that is your life directing it toward something good and meaningful in your relationships.

If You Have to Tell Someone You Are Something

If you have to tell someone you are something, then you probably are not. Instead, let your actions show people who and what you are. Too often, we tell people *what* we are, the human doing, and we fail to show them *who* we are, the human being. Only when they know the human being will there be the trust to build relationships and explore opportunities with the "human doing.

Show—don't tell. That is the best way to inform someone that you are something and to relate to them.

Gifts for Your Children

What are the gifts you are giving your children? One gift is to give them responsibility for their choices regarding what they do and how they behave. Let them experience the consequences, good or bad. They will learn that they can't talk their way out of problems that their behavior caused. Learning responsibility is a foundational gift for a good life.

Secondly, give them the gift of independence. Let them go, without your control, to make their own choices and experience either a victory or a defeat. As a result, they will learn to think and act independently for themselves. In turn, this will build their self-esteem and give them the confidence to move forward to embrace better future opportunities.

And there is a gift for you, the parent. Relationally, they are more likely to appreciate you for supporting them on their life path instead of trying to control it.

Difficult Times

All of us experience difficult times. To endure them mentally and emotionally in a better place, you must cultivate and have a deep belief in yourself and that you are here to fulfill a purpose. Purpose has many aspects, including keeping you focused on the road ahead. What goals do you want to achieve? Who are the people you love? Who loves you? What project or causes are you passionate about?

Difficult times are like sailing the stormy seas. They can knock us off course. But knowing your purpose provides the necessary fuel and serves as a compass and rudder to guide you over and beyond your difficulties. Purpose also moves you closer to the safe harbor that holds your success and happiness.

Baggage

Baggage—all of us have it! Baggage is the accumulation of our negative past experiences with people, circumstances, and things. Carry too much baggage, and it is impossible to find happiness in our relationships. One of the keys to becoming a better baggage handler of your own experiences is finding people who love you and help you unpack it.

Unpacking could be long conversations, active listening, or creating new experiences to replace those unwanted experiences of the past. Only when you unpack your baggage can you identify it. Once identified, you can take steps to minimize its influence and the weight it brings to your life. When you do, your self-esteem will soar, and your relationships will improve.

Why? You have decided to no longer be anchored to the past and have decided to use the past as a learning experience instead of a hammer that pounds you down.

See the Good, Find the Good

Every day consciously see the good in your life. Be grateful for it. Gratitude is the magnet that attracts good things and people into your life. Be a good finder in your relationships. Find the good. This is the foundation for solid relationships.

Seasonal People

Seasonal people come into our lives for a reason. They may appear briefly at a particular time or place. Like the seasons, they add value, but they come and go. Nature knows how to let go of one season so it can move into another. So likewise, we must learn to let go of relationships with seasonal people that no longer serve us. Only when we let go can we grow.

If It Fits, Keep It

Many of us have made the mistake of trying to change other people. Think about how hard it is to change yourself. When people enter your life, be as honest as possible about where they fit into your life based on *who* they are. Don't base it on who you want them to be. To have better and lasting relationships, learn about who a person is. When you do, you will make more correct decisions about who fits into your life and how. And you'll be happier for it.

Peace

You can drive yourself crazy trying to figure out what goes on with other people in your relationships. You can put them under your microscope and examine them in great detail and still not come up with definitive answers. This makes you even more frustrated and not only hurts you, but it can damage the other relationships you have in your life.

The next time you see yourself going down this path, which all of us do, step back. Some things will always remain a mystery. Further dissection and examination create more upset and discomfort. Instead, look at what you have learned and how it can move you forward in your relationships. This will bring you peace. Why? The key to peace is to live and to accomplish in the present. This brings you a sense of worth and value. Peace is not about spending your energy on the past and things you cannot change.

Procrastination

Procrastination, not doing the right thing on a timely basis by others in your relationships, can be deadly. Why? When you fail to do the right thing by others, you let the enemy of complacency, which breeds distrust and doubt, take over your relationships. Don't procrastinate! Fight complacency and the enemies of complacency: mistrust and doubt. Here's the question: Will it make any more sense tomorrow than it does today in your relationships to do the right thing by others?

Interested and Interesting

To make more friends be genuinely interested in other people instead of getting other people interested in you. Do you want better relationships? Be interested, not interesting! Always put your focus on being interested in others. That is what will make you interesting to them.

Keep Happy

Your happiness and the joy that comes from it are the antidotes to the challenges and difficulties life presents all of us. To create happiness and joy, always be a good "finder." First, find the good, no matter what, in people, your relationships, and situations. Next, express gratitude every day for the good in your life. Your focus on the positive as you go through life builds the muscles needed to continue growing, overcoming challenges, and having more successful relationships.

Friends

One friend who is there for your down moments and tears is more valuable than having many friends who only know you when you are smiling. Support and friendship are easy when things are great and you are smiling. Understanding and support from your friends when things are challenging, complex, and tearful enable you to overcome obstacles, get unstuck, and move forward. These friends have a priceless relationship value.

Pessimists and Optimists

Pessimists have a keen eye for what is wrong and what won't work, dominating their thinking. Whereas explorers who discover new worlds, teachers who improve the lives of the underprivileged, researchers who discover cures for diseases, and doctors who develop new methods for improving our health are all optimists. These people saw a problem—a negative—and determined to turn it into a positive.

Within every problem is the solution for something positive. If you focus on what is negative, you will sail the ship of your life from one storm to another. You will be stuck in a state of constant turbulence that is draining and de-energizing.

Focus on the positive, where you want your ship to sail to. Focus on what can be, not on what is. Be an optimist. Make the adjustments and deal with the problem, as positive people do, and you will guide your life to calmer, safer waters.

Life Will Test You

Life will test you. Choose to meet and pass the test. It is the only way you get stronger. There are hundreds of paths up the mountain of life, all leading to the same place, to your success and fulfillment. Just get started. It doesn't matter which path you take. Along the way to the top, you will be strong enough from walking and climbing to change course and to take another path if necessary.

Sometimes you may have to take a detour. Or, when presented with an opportunity, to be strong enough to seize it. In the process of walking and climbing, you'll become stronger and wiser from your experiences. Your conditioning, experience, and focus will keep you moving toward the top. Keep walking. Keep climbing. Keep experiencing. Those are the steps to success.

The Cocoon and Your Success

When you feel wrapped in by your circumstances, actions, or relationships, it might look like the darkness will never go away. Always remember the caterpillar. The caterpillar must go into a dark place, the cocoon, where it can't see the bright side of the life waiting for him, nor the growth of its wings.

Your personal development happens in the dark, on the inside. Nobody sees it. Like the caterpillar, you challenge yourself to grow to get to the light. And that is where the caterpillar becomes a butterfly. When you get to the light, like the caterpillar who turns into a beautiful butterfly, you will develop wings to fly to new possibilities in all areas of life.

 **KEY TAKEAWAYS**

✓ Be mindful of the supplies carried in your life's backpack.

✓ Responsibility is the greatest gift you can give your children.

✓ Rejoice in the success of others.

✓ A significant difference between a pessimist and an optimist is the object of their focus.

✓ Life has tests. Determine to pass them by adjusting your course or taking a detour.

CHAPTER 5

The Story of the Frog and the Scorpion

RELATIONSHIPS WILL BE DISASTROUS without awareness of what is good for you and what is not. The people we meet are not necessarily bad. But they, very often, are not a good fit. They are not a good fit because they cannot be TRUSTED. The following story highlights a problem most of us encounter. You somehow believe that you can change someone. And, this one belief, your ability to change someone, is an invitation into a relationship that will ultimately fail and very often cause you misery.

The Story

The frog and the scorpion appeared at the bank of the river at the same time. The frog is about to jump in and swim to the other side. The scorpion sees what is happening and engages the frog in conversation.

"Mr. Frog—I am a scorpion and cannot swim. Would you be kind enough to let me hop on your back, swim across the river, and deposit me on the other side? I would be grateful."

The frog looks at the scorpion and says, "No way. Scorpions sting frogs and kill them. I'd be out there, halfway, you would sting me, and I would drown."

The Scorpion looks at the frog and says, "Mr. Frog, you are not using your frog brain; you are not thinking. If I sting you out there, halfway, you will drown, and then I'd drown. I'm not interested in committing suicide. I'm just interested in getting to the other side. Please do me the favor."

The frog thinks about it and says, "Okay, that makes sense."

The scorpion hops on the frog's back. The frog starts swimming across the river. Sure enough, halfway across the river, the scorpion stings the frog. They are now both in the water and are about to go down for the third time. The frog cannot believe what is happening.

"Why did you do that? I am about to drown and die, and so are you. So why did you do that?"

The scorpion replied: "Because I am a scorpion!"

Get to know, like, and trust people for their core character, not their appearances and what they say they are. Character and the values that come with it are what truly matter. Only when those are right can you build trust and the potential for lasting relationships.

Additional Observations from
The Relationship Zoo

Be Happy Now

Happiness in your relationships is not something you put off. Are you waiting for the right circumstances or events to bring happiness to you and your relationships? Stop! Start designing your life for happiness in the present.

Happiness is not an amount. It is how you choose to experience life, and it will affect the quality of your relationships. Choose to create good experiences. Learn to design happiness into your life today. It will create positive momentum in your life to move you on a path to be all that you can be.

Grit and Resilience

Grit and resilience are the most significant contributors to success. Research has found that these two attributes are the most important. Your IQ is not the determining factor. Suppose you have a high IQ but don't have grit, the ability to grind it out, and resilience, the inner strength to overcome adversity. In that case, you won't have the success of which you are capable.

To have ongoing relationships where you build value, you must have grit and resilience. Even the best relationships will have times that test your patience, love, and understanding. So, develop your grit and resilience muscles. The resistance they force you to overcome develops the muscles that will allow you to succeed and grow in your life and relationships.

Believe in Somebody's Belief in You

Sometimes you have to believe in somebody's belief in you until your belief in yourself kicks in. The power and influence of your associations, i.e., your relationships, are incredible. Hang around people who genuinely believe in you. The ones who believe in you may praise you occasionally, but they will do something more meaningful. They will always encourage you. The encouragement of others in your relationships is a powerful fuel that will drive your engine of success while creating deeper and more meaningful and personal bonds. Believe in somebody's belief in you.

You Have Power Over Your Mind

"You have power over your mind—not outside events. Realize this, and you will find strength." (Marcus Aurelius) Conceive it. What do you want in your relationships? Believe it. Believe that you can have the relationships you desire. Achieve it. Go out, and here's the key: Become the person you must be to have the relationships you want. It all starts with the power you have over your mind. For better relationships, use the power you have over your mind to conceive it, believe it, and then achieve it.

Inaction

Inaction is the breeding ground for indifference, indecision, doubt, worry, and over-caution. These are based on fear and will zap you of your confidence and courage. Action cures fear or, at the very least, gets you on track to conquer it.

My mother used to tell me that nothing happens within the four walls of our home. You can't go out and build meaningful, new relationships and possible opportunities staying at home. Home was an excellent place to think. Yet, thinking alone does not build self-esteem. She always encouraged me to turn my thinking into action. Turn it into action where I position myself to meet people.

And with action, that's where the miracle process of what life has to offer was opened to me. It was extended through new relationships. Take action! Build new relationships and possibilities.

Your Most Important Decision

Prolific writer Francois-Marie Arouet, aka Voltaire, wrote, *"The most important decision you make is to be in a good mood."* Why is this true? Because how you choose to feel about yourself and your world is projected to others. Their response will either elevate you or depress you.

Unfortunately, stuff happens to all of us. You can either be other-directed, outer-directed, or inner-directed. Control your own weather. Take charge of your mood. Decide to be inner-directed. It will make things better for you and your relationships.

Meet Better People-Become the Right Person

If you desire better relationships, start with yourself. When you become the right person, an improved version of yourself, you will attract better people into your life. Become the best you! When you do, you will find that more quality people are attracted to you.

Connection

Connection with others is about heart-to-heart. Interestingly, there is a common phrase that is used when talking about connecting. You must reach, speak to, or touch others' "hearts and minds." It does not say "minds and hearts." There is a reason. Reach people first emotionally on a heart level, and their minds will be much more open to you and what you have to say. A heart-to-heart connection is the foundation for more solid relationships.

Dog Relationships

I once heard someone say that "If I could be half the person my dog is, I could be two or three times the human that I am." Dogs are very capable of giving unconditional love and support. They don't care what has gone on in your day, good, bad, or indifferent. They love you regardless of people, circumstances, and things. In human relationships, it is more complicated. If and when you find the opportunities to give unconditional love and support, it deepens your relationships while enlarging your world and, most importantly, you.

Always Remember How People Make You Feel

For all of us, what we remember and how we remember it can get muddled over time. In your relationships, it's been shown that you won't remember exactly what was said very often. And, unless it was truly bizarre, you won't remember how someone behaved.

Yet, there is one thing that you will remember accurately, how that person made you feel. So, start today by focusing on how you make others feel. That's what they will remember about you. As others feel better about you, you will feel elevated and experience more positivity in your relationships.

Obstacles

Obstacles are the tests in the school that are your relationships. When a test shows up in your relationships, do the best you can to welcome it. Why? Within the obstacle—the test—lies the answer to what you must do to move things forward. To have better relationships understand and know that the obstacle is the way to determine what is best for you and the relationship. Welcome obstacles!

Apologies and Changed Behavior

The best apology is a consistent and lasting change in behavior. Why? Changed behavior that is sincere and consistent over time shows you genuinely care about others and value them. Changed behavior emphasizes "we" instead of "me" because you appreciated someone's response enough to cause you to change, and they see it. The best apologies are reflected in your changed behavior.

Changed behavior emphasizes "we" instead of "me"...

Happiness in Relationships

Happiness in relationships can come in the moments we spend with others. Yet, moments of happiness come and go. So, to have long-term satisfaction, recognize and appreciate what you do have in your relationships that you are grateful for. Gratitude can take you out of the valley in a relationship and place you and the relationship on a mountain top. And that is something that will bring you happiness.

Follow the Crowd? Walk Alone?

When you follow the crowd, you will go only as far as the crowd. When you walk alone, you're leading and more likely to find yourself in places you have never been before. So step out of the crowd and be all that you can be. It will not only make you different. It will become the first step to becoming more, to being better.

Bad Vibes

Your feelings are valid. When you encounter someone, you can either feel good, bad, or indifferent. So, what do you do? There is a part of you that wants to connect with other people. And, if you get a bad vibe when you connect, your innate curiosity may cause you to get deeper into a relationship than what is good for you.

Is it curiosity? Or is it your desire to help a person fix their situation that is driving you? Understand what is causing you to override the bad vibes. Once you understand this, you are less likely to be in unhealthy, unhappy relationships that drain you of your gifts and talents.

Talk to Yourself—Talk to Others

The next time you say to yourself, "I have to do........." (fill in the blank), then remember this: Your self-talk is critical to your energy level. And your energy level is the key to what you will accomplish.

Instead of saying, "I have to do" or "I have to," say this: "I get to do......." and fill in the blank. "I get to do........." will have a positive effect on your energy. Try it. The positive energy from "I get to do........" will serve you well in your work and your relationships.

What are you saying when you talk to yourself? It is what you will say when you speak to others. Think about how your language is impacting your relationships.

Be Here Now

Be here now in your relationships. Yesterday is past, and it is best, unless necessary, to keep it there. Only by keeping the past in the past can you give today your best shot. Be here now. Be in the present. Look back too much to yesterday, and you will miss the present relationship opportunities right in front of you. Looking backward will never take you forward. Learn from the past to help you move forward today, but don't dwell there.

Give your focus today to those people in your life. Be here now and give people the most important gift, your attention. No one ever feels good in a relationship if they feel they are being taken for granted. Be here now!

Wishbone and Backbone

Are you wishing, hoping, and praying for better relationships? Part of the challenge in connecting with others can happen if they are unclear about who you are and what you stand for. If they are unclear, this creates distance, and they are less likely to connect with you on a deeper level.

Very often, you can go into a relationship with a wishbone instead of a backbone. A wishbone is about how you wish things will turn out. But a backbone gives others a clear picture of who you are and whether or not the relationship has possibilities. A backbone gives others something genuine to connect with within you.

All of us have wishbones. Combine the wishbone with a backbone, and others will connect with the authentic you, bringing you opportunities for greater happiness and fulfillment.

Your Environment

The environment you choose with your relationships will shape you. Why? Because you will become more like the people you most associate with. Be careful! Everything matters. You can drift into stormy seas when you don't think everything matters—especially in your relationships.

Look at the sea you are swimming in. Then look at who you are swimming with. Finally, ask yourself what influence my environment and associations are having on me? Is this acceptable? Too much influence is undue influence.

Who Truly Matters?

The American poet, Edna Wheeler Wilcox, wrote, *"There's one sad truth in life I've found while journeying east and west. The only folks we really wound are those we love the best. We flatter those we scarcely know. We please the fleeting guest. And deal full many a thoughtless blow to those who love us best."*

Don't give all your attention to the people you think are very important and miss those who truly matter, those who love you the best. To move toward greater peace of mind in your relationships, be mindful of who truly matters.

Seasons And People

People come into your life in two ways. They are either there for a season or there for a lifetime. Never mix your seasonal people into your lifetime expectations.

In your life, you have seasons. And people will show up during a season for a reason. They can help you temporarily move forward in fulfilling your lifetime expectations. Like the seasons, they come and go—except, unlike nature, you have a choice as to whether or not to keep them. Nature teaches us about growth as she moves from one season to another.

You must learn to recognize seasonal relationships and to let go of them when they no longer serve you. Just like the tree that lets go of its leaves every Fall to grow more prominently in the Spring, you can only grow when you let go of the leaves in your life, the seasonal people.

 **KEY TAKEAWAYS**

✓ Don't put off being happy for another day.

✓ Offering unconditional love and support in a relationship will enlarge your world.

✓ Instead of saying, "I *have* to," rephrase it to say, "I *get* to." It will serve you well.

✓ The best apology is demonstrated in changed behavior.

✓ Life has seasons. Some seasons bring pruning, and some bring growth.

CHAPTER 6

What is Being Mirrored to You?

WHAT IS BEING MIRRORED back to you in your relationships? Long ago, in a small, far away village, there was a place known as "The House of 1,000 Mirrors." After learning about this place, a small, happy little dog decided to visit. When the dog arrived, he bounced happily up the stairs to the doorway with his ears lifted high and his tail wagging as fast as it could.

To his great surprise, he found himself staring at 1,000 other happy little dogs with their tails wagging just as fast as his was. He smiled a great smile and was answered with 1,000 great smiles, just as warm and friendly. As he left the House, he thought to himself, "This is a wonderful place. I will come back and visit it often."

In the same village, another little dog, who was not quite as happy as the first one, decided to visit the House. He slowly climbed the stairs and hung his head low as he looked in the door. When he saw 1,000 unfriendly dogs staring back at him, he growled at them and was horrified to see 1,000 little dogs growling back at him. As he left, he thought to himself, "That is a horrible place, and I will never go back there again."

All the faces in the world are mirrors. Our relationships are mirrors of who we are in the eyes of others. What kind of reflections are you seeing in the faces of the people in your life?

Additional Observations from
The Relationship Zoo

Be Kind or Be Right?

In an ideal world, it would be nice if we could be both kind and correct all the time. That is not reality. For better relationships, keep kindness at the forefront. Regardless of culture, kindness is the universal language that every human being understands. Actions of kindness will open doors, while relationships that focus on being right will close them. Kindness can be your path to better relationships based on *what* is right, not *who* is right.

Be the Best You

When you get tired, learn to rest. Resting is not quitting. Rest is necessary for personal growth and high performance. Without enough rest, you can become too tired, feeling like you can't go on and quit. Rest is necessary to protect your most valuable asset, you! Focus on your self-preservation. When you do, you will discover opportunities to be the best that you can be. And it will improve your relationships. Why? Only the best "you" can be the best for others.

Weather

Your attitude is the weather in your life. What do people feel when they are with you? What do they forecast your weather to be before they see you? You do have control over the weather, your attitude. So, bring brightness and warmth in your weather to others. The only way to bring brightness, warmth, and sunshine to others and your life is first to give it. Only then are you more likely to receive the same from others.

What if you have a day, as all of us do, where you just aren't feeling it? Your attitude just isn't there. First, recognize all the things you have to be grateful for. Second, go out and serve someone. It could be as simple as opening a door when someone is carrying a package. It could be letting that car into your lane that needs to get on the freeway.

Look for opportunities to do good. When you do, it will improve your attitude, your weather, because you have done something good for others.

Choices

I bought a bag of chips the other day, and as I opened it, I was reminded in a humorous way that air (which there was a lot of inside the bag) is not free. In reality, the air that truly matters, the air we breathe, is free. It is what we choose to do as we breathe the free air, with our time, resources, and, ultimately, the consequences of those not free choices. Use your time and resources wisely, and you will breathe freely.

Fulfilling Lives

People who lead and live the most fulfilling lives are the ones who are always happy with what they have. They are grateful. Their primary focus is on their blessings, not on what they don't have. You can never feel fulfilled if you come from the viewpoint of always lacking something. Gratitude fills you up positively. That is what fulfillment is about, the positive. Be grateful. You will feel fulfilled. You will rejoice in what you have. And it will allow you to connect positively with others.

Thoughts To Improve Your Relationships

Live authentically. Love without neediness. Listen to understand not to win. And speak in a manner to encourage people to listen to you and to have a conversation. In all of these, you cannot be better with and for others if how you are thinking and acting ultimately drives others from your life.

You Are Responsible for Your Happiness

When others want you to feel bad about a decision you made that upsets them remember this: You are not responsible for their happiness. You are responsible for your own. So, if anyone wants you to be miserable because of their unhappiness with you, they do not, for starters, need to be part of your life.

Anyone who defines their happiness by *your* unhappiness needs to have a limited role or no role in your life. They are a cancer. Since there is no chemotherapy for cancerous relationships, very often, the best option is to perform mental and emotional surgery and remove them.

Grounded or Flying?

Your attitude about yourself and your world is what you project on others. For example, do you have a flight plan, an attitude that makes others want to lift you and fly above the clouds? Or is your attitude causing others to keep you grounded.

For your life to take off, have a flight plan that sees the value in others and lifts them. When you see value in others, they will want to raise you to fly above the clouds. And, above the clouds is where you will see more blue skies and sunshine on the flight that is your life.

Every Dog That Barks

In building a solid foundation and a good life, there are many distractions. These distractions are like dogs that bark. Suppose you give attention to every dog that barks. In that case, it will distract you from your priorities and, ultimately, your ability to accomplish. Relationships can be the same way. Suppose you encounter people who are, more often than not, negative or who are always inviting drama into their lives, even though they don't realize it. In that case, it is time to move on.

These relationships are like barking dogs because they provide continuous distractions. They take you off purpose and stop you on your path to becoming more like a person on their way to success and fulfillment.

Care Enough to Be There

How do you make a difference in someone's life? You may be rich, intelligent, and likable. That is good. But to make a difference when someone needs you, care enough to be there. You can be well off financially. You can learn a great deal. You can explore and try many things. You can accomplish great deeds. And people like you.

Yet, if you care enough to be there for those who matter, that is the difference that will be remembered through all that you have accomplished. How much you care is reflected in the difference you can make in the lives of others. It is your most lasting and human legacy.

Positive Attention

What is positive attention? It is paying value to others by finding and acknowledging the good in them. Too often, we see the good yet fail to acknowledge it. You must speak your positive thoughts for them to be genuine acknowledgments that convey positive attention. Positive attention is the key not only to improved productivity but to deeper connections and better relationships. So today, acknowledge the goodness in someone!

Let Go of Your Right to be Offended

If you want to keep your peace and have more stable and harmonious relationships, let go of your right to be offended. Today, with social media, people's inclination to be offended or to find anything offensive has skyrocketed. Bad things, offensive things have existed throughout history.

But now, with social media, offended people have a platform. Being offended is a form of anger. Anyone's anger is valid. What we choose to do with it or how we express it is the question. Getting offended quickly chills conversations, causes people to tiptoe around you, and, worst of all, distances people from you.

It is hard to have good relationships if people realize that you get easily offended. After all, who wants to get close to a person whose anger is about ready to bubble over. Stop being offended. More often than not, being offended is founded on our desire to show that we are someone. Also, it can temporarily give us some control over others.

Let go of being offended and keep your peace. It is a mistake to think that others should be or feel the way we think they should. When you let go of your right to be offended, you are on a path to more stable and deeper relationships.

When you let go of your right to be offended, you are on a path to more stable and deeper relationships.

The Two Most Important Days

The first important day in your life is the day you were born. After all, until you arrive on this Earth, you cannot begin to take the journey to discover the second most important day. That is the day you find out "why" you are here. The answer to "why" you are here is critical to your happiness and sense of well-being.

Discover your purpose and calling. It may take many years, and that is okay. Your purpose or calling will tell you "why" you are here. When you are clear about "why," you will attract the people who will support you. The day you know "why" is the day that you will begin to "fly" higher in your relationships and life.

Drama

Drama does not show up in your life on quiet, little cat feet. It usually comes by invitation, except you don't realize you are inviting it in. Drama either comes from within, comes from an outside event, or another person. All three of these can be mixed to cause drama.

Take a look at the origin of most of your drama. Is it your thoughts? Is it from discomforting outside events? Or is it from another person? Then, of course, some drama just shows up, and it cannot be avoided. But what about the drama you invite in? Do something about it. When you do, you will be on a path to greater peace in your relationships and life.

Talent and Comparison

Like the animals in the forest, we all have talents and skills. To survive and thrive, animals know who they are and value it. It is instinctual. When the squirrel sees a fox, it doesn't think, "*I wish I were a bear.*" No. The squirrel knows it can climb trees, and the fox cannot.

Yet, as a human being, you have to discover your talents and skills through experience, trial, and error. You can easily get disheartened in the process because, unlike the animals in the forest, you compare yourself to others and find yourself lacking. Too often, in comparing, we *overvalue* what we are not and *undervalue* what we are. Instead, value who you are; it will help your self-esteem and improve your relationships.

Cocooning

When you feel wrapped in the dark and despair of finding the light, remember the caterpillar. The caterpillar must live in the darkness of the cocoon to grow its wings. Your personal development happens in the dark, on the inside, in your cocoon. Nobody sees it. Like the caterpillar, you must accept the challenge to grow to get to the light, where you can develop your wings to fly.

Purpose

Work for a cause. Live your life to express. You will receive applause for your work when you do, and others will be impressed with your life. Your absence will be noticed. Work or focus on something bigger than yourself.

Have a "go give" attitude toward others in all that you do. What you give to others is what they appreciate about you. When you are not present to offer what others appreciate about you, your absence will be felt. What are you giving?

Words

Mixing bad words with a bad mood is not healthy for you and your relationships. You will have opportunities to change your mood, your attitude. But you will never get the chance to replace the words you speak.

The words you speak today are heard by the ears attached to the mouth that will repeat them tomorrow. What story do you want others to be telling about you? It is much easier to forgive or overlook someone's bad mood, let alone forget about it when bad words don't get in the way. So be careful of the words you choose.

Perspective

Sometimes initially, we are touched by something good, yet it can end up being wrong. Another time we may encounter a negative, and it turns out to be positive. The point is that your initial perspective may change. So be ready to change your perspective. It is a must if you are going to be happy and have success in life.

I picked some beautiful wildflowers, my initial perspective, behind my home. On the way to the house, I was stung by a bee that I did not see among the flowers. My perspective changed. The flowers were still pretty, but my desire to pick more of them disappeared.

With the swelling from the bee sting and its allergic reaction, I started to itch. As I went to put some lotion on my arm, I discovered that there was very little left in the tube. So, I went to the store and purchased more. The itching subsided.

My perspective changed again. It turned out that the bee sting, which was bothering me, caused me to solve another problem, a lack of lotion to treat the itching. And, ironically, now I became grateful for the bee sting. For without it, I would not have had the ointment to treat the itching from bee stings, poison ivy, and insect bites when I go out in the woods.

Life is a learning experience for all of us. In your relationships, keep learning. You will guide yourself on a better path that finds fewer bee stings and more flowers without the bees when you do.

Overcome Fear: Turn Thinking into Action

Action breeds self-confidence and courage. By taking action, you have decided doubts, worries, and fear will not rule you. Yes, they will be there. But their power over you will be diminished because you have decided to act to overcome them. Your focus is now on action, not on doubt, worry, and fear.

Action, although there is the risk of failure, is the only way to overcome fear. The miracle process of life is when you turn your thoughts into action and discover what life truly has to offer. So go out and get busy and overcome. It will help your confidence, your courage, your results, and your relationships.

 **KEY TAKEAWAYS**

✓ Resting is a critical component in being the absolute best YOU.

✓ Your attitude is like a flight plan that determines the course of your life.

✓ Focus on who you *are* instead of who you *are not*.

✓ Having a purpose in life allows you to focus on something bigger than yourself.

✓ Turning your thoughts into action brings possibilities for opportunity

CHAPTER 7

Good Teams Make for Better Relationships

AN OUT-OF-TOWN MOTORIST drove his car into a ditch in a desolate area in rural Ohio. His car was stuck and could not move. Luckily, a local farmer came along, saw the situation, and offered to help. He told the out-of-towner he would be back in an hour.

The farmer went to his farmhouse up on the hill and returned with his big, strong horse named Buddy. The motorist was perplexed but did not say anything. He was thinking the whole time that there was no way that this would work.

The man watched the farmer as he hitched Buddy up with a rope to the car and yelled, "Pull, Nellie, pull." Buddy didn't move. Then the farmer hollered, "Pull, Buster, pull." Buddy didn't respond.

The motorist had now lost all hope that his car would be pulled out of the ditch.

Once more, the farmer commanded in a loud voice, "Pull, Jennie, pull." Nothing. Then the farmer said nonchalantly, in a loud voice, "Pull, Buddy, pull." And the horse quickly dragged the car out of the ditch.

The motorist was astonished, most appreciative, and very curious. He asked the farmer why he called his horse, Buddy, by the wrong name three times. The farmer said, "Oh, Buddy is almost deaf, and he is blind. If he thought he was the only one pulling, he wouldn't even try!"

Great power can come from within you when you believe you are part of a team. Be part of a team in your relationships. Together, you can accomplish something bigger and better in the right relationships than if you were on your own.

Additional Observations from
The Relationship Zoo

Speaking and Listening

The words you speak reflect what you know or think you know. On the other hand, if you listen and are a good listener, you may learn something new. Be a great listener. There are several benefits. When you listen with intent, you pay value to others, learning what they are thinking.

Then your responses to what they are saying will be more on point, showing them that you value their thoughts. When you appreciate others' thoughts, it leads to improved communication, better teams, and deeper relationships.

Living Well and Longer

A Tibetan proverb advises, *"The secret to living well and longer: eat half, walk double, laugh triple and love without measure."* Eat what you need. Exercise. See the humor in yourself and life. And love without measure because you have gratitude for all the good and blessings in your life. When you do all of these, you will find more inner peace, experience more happiness in your relationships, and increase your odds of living well and longer.

What Matters

In your behavior and what you say, look at the response of the people around you. There is wisdom in understanding, that for the most part, those who mind you don't matter while those that matter in your life don't mind you.

You will find that the people of little or no consequence in your life generally don't appreciate or understand you. The people of consequence are the ones that energize, promote, respect, and understand you. Find those people who get you. They matter. For greater fulfillment and happiness, weave them into the fabric that is your life.

What Cannot Live

We cannot live without air. And love cannot live without trust.

There You Are!

The first impression you give to others in a new or an existing relationship shows your attitude about others. And they will pick up on it! When you encounter someone, are you saying to them, "Here I am!" with your attitude and words? Or are you communicating with your attitude words, "There you are!"?

Are you about "me" or about "we"? There are times to be about "me" and times to be about "we." For more positive encounters, focus on appreciating others with a "There you are" attitude.

Causes

All of us have causes we support. However, the one cause all of us have in common, at the most fundamental level, is to promote our survival. And once you master survival, then you will want to embrace the cause of thriving. Thriving is what you can give to and share with others.

Your life is your cause. What you share and give to others is how they will see you and your life regardless of obstacles, setbacks, and triumphs. So, live a life of sharing and giving to others while taking care of yourself. When you do, the cause that is your life will leave a legacy of triumph, leaving others better for their experience with you.

Appreciation

Appreciate others, and you will find many other people are drawn to you. Why? Appreciation bestows on others a sense of gratitude because of their presence in your life. This is attractive not only to them but to everyone who has personal interaction with you. Appreciation will enhance and expand your relationships. It will enlarge your life.

Acceptance and Forgiveness

You don't have to accept someone's behavior or trust them. But you must forgive them so that you can move beyond them and go forward in your other relationships. Otherwise, you carry that negativity into your other relationships.

Forgiveness is the necessary mindset to start the healing process with the most important relationship you have—the one with yourself. But, more importantly, forgiveness lessens the debilitating weight of negativity and allows you to keep moving forward in the relationships you truly value.

Your Power Is Over Your Mind

For a better relationship with yourself, remember this: You have power over your mind. You cannot control others. You cannot control outside events. But you can always go to your one source of strength, your mind, and how you choose to see things.

Control your mind, and you will control your perspective. Conceive it. Believe it. These only come from one source, the power over your mind. After your mind conceives it and believes it, you are now positioned to go out and achieve it.

Interruptions

Interruptions in life allow us to appreciate and enjoy more of the good things that are being interrupted. How? When your sleep is interrupted, you appreciate a good uninterrupted sleep. When your health is interrupted, you value and enjoy good health even more.

The truth is that it is difficult to appreciate how much you have that is good until an interruption occurs and either alters a good situation or causes it to disappear. Therefore, every day take a moment to appreciate all the good in your life. Then, when something good is interrupted, you can reference all the other good that you have. This will keep you moving forward with the positive attitude necessary to overcome present situations, maintain good relationships, and move forward on your path to the future you desire.

Let Go of Your Need to Be Right

The only things you truly have control over are your feelings and your thoughts about those feelings. Yet, in relationships, we can often try to control the relationship by emphasizing how right we are to the other person.

Let go of your need to be correct. Instead, pick up your need to understand others. Serve them by being sincere in understanding them. When you put them first by understanding them, they are more likely to put you first. But that only happens if you let go of your need to be right.

Never Underestimate Your Power

Serve others and leave them better for having crossed your path.

The smallest act of kindness, the tiniest act of caring, your smile, listening to a concern, and giving positive acknowledgments all have the power and potential to turn a life around. Give these as an act of service to others. Serve others and leave them better for having

79

crossed your path. This is a great power to use and will leave a lasting, positive legacy. Never underestimate your power.

Movement and Success

Successful people understand one thing. When sitting down, you can't stumble onto something good. Good things come into people's lives who are on the move. They don't depend on luck. They understand that movement brings opportunities for success, that either they discover or that find them.

People who don't move hope they get lucky and that something good will fall into their lives. Position yourself for good things. Be movable, and you will increase the likelihood of stumbling onto something better in your relationships and life.

Pessimism

Pessimism is a jail for the human spirit. When in your mental prison, you can't discover new things, develop new skills, and most importantly, you cannot serve others with a positive mindset. Also, pessimism and its focus on the negative will take the ship that is your life, your relationships, and sink it. Alter your course. Focus on the positive, where you want your ship to sail to. Deal with the negative, the pessimism, as a learning experience. Do as positive people do. Steer the rudder of your ship toward a favorable destination with calmer seas.

Should

"Should" is a perfectly good word when used correctly. We should be moral. We should be honest. And there are many others you can add to the list. But when we use "should" to make a point of something that we would like to see a person do, it can become a distancer and separator in relationships.

When you tell someone that they "Should have............" and you can fill in the blanks, you are using the word should in a way that puts guilt on the other person for not doing something to your liking. You are also creating an obligation in their minds to conform to your way of thinking.

Should, when personalized, is about guilt and obligation. How well do you feel when someone uses "should" on you? The word should is a divider, more often than not, when used on a person. Also, the tone with which it is used causes it to come across as criticism.

Be careful how you use the word should. For better relationships, stop "should"-ing on others. Also, stop "should"-ing on yourself. No one thrives with extra guilt and obligation.

Toxic People

If someone in your life is happy because they make you unhappy, you need to delete them. Anyone who defines their happiness by your misery is toxic to you. They are a contagious disease and will cause you to carry *their* sickness and unhappiness into *your* life and the lives of the people you touch. Let go of them. When you do, you and the people in your life will get well.

Personal Responsibility

What is personal responsibility in your relationships? It is not trying to change the other person. All of us know how hard it is to change ourselves, let alone others. Personal responsibility is your guide to having better relationships because it demands that you be willing to some degree to change yourself, alter your thinking, and adapt. Every relationship—weak or strong—has a foundation on adaptability. Changing your thinking is the first step to adaptability and to taking personal responsibility in your relationships.

The Earth-The Wind-Trust

Trust can be like the Earth, always there. Or it can be like the wind—here one moment and gone the next, never to return.

Procrastination and Prevention

Procrastination is like living your life on continuous credit. But, in the end, you always have to pay the bill. And the bill is larger because interest has accumulated.

Procrastination lets weeds grow in your garden of success. Eventually, the weeds take over the garden. Don't wait! Start pulling the weeds out today.

Prevention, the daily weeding of your garden so it can remain beautiful and functional, is the enemy of procrastination. Prevention says, "I will take care of it now, so I don't have to take care of something bigger later." Every day pull out your weeds of procrastination in your business, life, and relationships.

The Language of Kindness

Kindness is a language of care and concern, regardless of culture. Even those who can't see, can't hear, or can't understand our language, can feel kindness. It is foundational to healthy relationships.

Kindness doesn't need an interpreter. It is about actions, facial and body expressions, words if they are understood, and touch. Every human being is connected by kindness because it is the worldwide expression of human caring.

Decisions That Upset Others

Have you ever felt bad about making a decision that upsets other people? All of us have. No one likes to feel bad. Yet, this, like many things we don't like, is self-inflicted.

To have a happier and more fulfilling life, we must understand that we are not responsible for the happiness of others. We are only responsible for our happiness. But, yes, all of us can do things that make others legitimately unhappy. And, depending on the situation, maybe we can do something about it.

But, too often, people try to control other people by making them believe that they, the other people, are responsible for their happiness. That is an unhappy place to be. Anyone who wants you to be unhappy for the sake of their happiness does not, for starters, need to be in your life.

Furthermore, anyone who defines their happiness by your misery is toxic to you. They are a contagious disease and cause you to carry their sickness and unhappiness into your life and the lives of the people you touch. So let go of these people, and you and your life will be better for it.

 **KEY TAKEAWAYS**

✓ Kindness is a language spoken worldwide.

✓ The word "should" divides when used in our expectations for others.

✓ Pessimism is a mental prison that limits your potential.

✓ When you are upset with yourself, focus your thoughts on something other than yourself.

✓ The people who *get* you are the ones who matter.

CHAPTER 8

Raise Your Level of Expectation for Yourself

THE FOLLOWING IS A STORY from my childhood where I learned first-hand what can happen when I give more and bring more value. What I received in that situation was more than I ever expected.

As a little boy, when my dad asked me to work around the house, I would try to find something else to do. I'd hide in the basement or find someone to play with. Eventually, he would find me and gently remind me of the unfinished chores.

In his way, he was teaching me responsibility. I wasn't ready, but he was patient. As I got a little older, we were cutting trees with an ax. It was hard work. I was so mad at having to do it. Here it was Saturday, and I was cutting down trees. This situation was not the portrait of the good life that I had in my twelve-year-old mind. I should have been playing with the other kids. I was so angry about having to do the job that I finished it long before he expected.

Next, I did the rest of the chores and other things that I hadn't been asked to complete. I picked up sticks in the yard and got the woodpile in order, which my dad usually handled.

When we sat down at lunch, he was smiling. He complimented me and recognized my accomplishments. In fact, I had done extra things so now he wouldn't have to spend the time. I had done more than what was asked for, more than what was expected, and it felt great.

There was nothing better than being recognized and appreciated by my dad. And, he said that what I had done reminded him of a story from his childhood.

The story was about a man who was upset that he didn't have any heat in the middle of winter. The man sat in front of the pot-bellied stove arguing with it and saying, "Give me the heat, then I will give you the wood."

My father pointed out that too many people go through life with the wrong attitude. He told me that I had to put something *in* before I would get something back *out*.

At that point, he paused and smiled again. He said, "Steve, you have really helped me a lot today. What I thought was going to take all day was finished by 11:00. Thank you. How would you like to go see the Yankees play the Red Sox this afternoon?"

I couldn't believe what I was hearing! We usually went to one major league baseball game a year. It was expensive, and we didn't have much money. I felt excitement, happiness, and euphoria colliding at the same time. I was going to be with my dad and do something I loved.

As we drove to the game, he told me again how much he appreciated my help and how it was always good to give more than expected. He told me when I give more than expected that the extra is an investment in my future.

Years later, I still think about that day. Little did I know that morning that giving more than expected would result in an afternoon and baseball game with my dad. Who knows the beautiful rewards life holds when you do a little extra?

Raise your level of expectation for yourself. Do it for yourself, and you will give more to others. When you give more than expected, you are positioning yourself to add value to yourself to enhance the possibilities for more meaningful and positive relationships.

Additional Observations from
The Relationship Zoo

Your Relationships Are an Echo

What signals, by your words and actions, are you sending to others? Are you generous and bring joy? When you join positively with others, you add value because you can now enlarge each other as a team. Are your words and actions genuinely productive? And, most importantly, are you interested in serving others by adding value to them and their lives? You may not be able to do all of these. But at least do some. When you do, your relationships will be better. Yes, your relationships are an echo. What you send out comes back!

Superiority?

Suppose you measure your relationships by your superiority to someone others. In that case, I can assure you that you are a taker and do not have good relationships. Why? You are consistently positioning yourself to show your superiority and to take someone down. Who wants to be around someone like this, let alone trust them?

When it comes to superiority, a much better focus is to become superior to your former self. After all, the only accurate measure of success is not wealth, power, fame, or position. It is the ratio between who you are and who you can become.

Approve of Yourself

Very often, criticism comes in the form of your self-talk. Maybe you have tried self-criticism for a long time and realize that it does not work. This is especially true in the area of your relationships. You talk about what you could have, would have, or should have done. These are about wishing or hoping you had done something differently.

Instead, focus on what you can do. Approve of yourself by focusing on the positives about yourself. Subconsciously, concentrate on the good you have done in the past or what you are doing well in the present. Approving of yourself leads you to have more positive energy in your relationships.

See the Best in Others

One thing that can diminish relationships is your inability to see the best in others. Of course, you don't have to wear rose-colored glasses and ignore negatives that could have a significant impact. But if you want to see how good a relationship can be, so both of you can get the most out of it, you must look for the best in others.

People love to be acknowledged for their goodness. When you give acknowledgment, it encourages the other person to live up to the good you see in them. Encourage others! See the best in them!

People love to be acknowledged for their goodness.

Beware of People Who Tell You That You Cannot Make a Difference

People who tell you that you cannot make a difference are those who themselves are afraid to take the initiative. They are also the ones who are fearful that you will be successful.

Those afraid to take the initiative let the enemies of fear, over-caution, or timidity rule them. And unfortunately, they are very often nice people.

Then some are afraid you will succeed. It would be best if you were much more careful with them. Very often, unhappy people are fearful because they are threatened by change or by your success. It is their low self-esteem that makes them jealous of others' successes. Know who you are dealing with in your relationships. When you do, you can make a difference!

Change

Here is a simple truth. If you cannot change your mind, then you do not have the power to change anything. Change requires that you first change your thinking. A shift in your thinking results in many positive outcomes. First, you now have the possibility of changing your habits. When you change your habits, you will then change your activity. When you change your activity, you will then change your results. And, when you change your results, it will ultimately change your life!

And all these changes in each area will change your relationships. The change in relationships will have a significant effect on your life. All change and your ability to change anything starts in your mind.

Painful Experiences

I was with my granddaughter at the playground, and she wanted to play on the monkey bars. Unfortunately, as a three-and-a-half-year-old, she was too small to have the strength to go from one bar to the next. So, I held her up to where she could grab the bar with both hands and then, while still holding her, had her release one of her hands from the bar and grab the next bar. As she let go, she moved forward and got excited about her progress.

Getting over or through painful experiences is like moving forward on the monkey bars. The only way you can move forward is to let go. The great secret to moving beyond painful experiences is to practice the art of letting go. When you let go, you don't forget what has happened. Instead, you let go by putting the painful experiences in the past and keeping them in the past.

When you do, their poisonous effect will be minimal on your present and future relationships. Let go, just like you were crossing the monkey bars, of the resentment, the anger, and the pain. Otherwise, you will create a present and a future remarkably similar to the past, filled with the painful experiences you are trying to get over.

The Pause

The pause can and will make your relationships much better. Practice pausing before making a judgment. Pause before you are about ready to tell someone what you think. When you wait, you will avoid behaving and talking in a way that you may regret for years.

We all are guilty of speeding in our thoughts and emotions, just like the car that goes too fast. But sadly, when we speed up, we increase the odds of having a crash. So, the next time you feel pressured into a quick reaction, take a moment—that is all it takes—to pause and reflect.

With this moment, you have given yourself the time to choose what you will say or how you will act, which usually results in a better response. A thoughtfully, considered response will move you forward in your relationships and enhance your life.

Who Believes in You?

Who do you surround yourself with? Are they dreamers or doers? Are they passionate about what they believe? Do they think things through? Again, there is no right or wrong here.

The critical question is this: How are the people with who you surround yourself influencing you? First, find people who believe in you. These are the people who see and appreciate your gifts and talents. Why?

People who believe in you and your gifts and talents are people who very often see in you what you don't see in yourself. These are the people who are most likely to affirm you, promote you and open the doors to opportunities that lead to a happier and more fulfilling life.

The people who believe in you are the ones who will help create the momentum that will carry you forward to new experiences and more significant accomplishments.

The Prescription for Unhappiness

If you want to be unhappy, constantly be comparing yourself to others. Someone always has it better, easier, etc. That's *their* highlight reel. And you keep playing the video of all your behind-the-scenes struggles. The comparison is never favorable, nor does it enhance your relationships. When you bring a diminished feeling about yourself into a relationship, it will have a negative impact.

So, what do you do? First, create your own highlight reel: your accomplishments and all you have to be grateful for. Next, go to work on yourself. Look at yourself today. And ask yourself, "Who do I want to become?" Only when you enlarge yourself, become more as a person, will you feel more secure and create a highlight reel that will bring positive energy to you and your relationships.

Life is Your Dance

Life is your dance where the steps and tempo can and will change. The challenge is to meet these changes and to be authentic, to remain true to yourself. As you move through your life, dance with gratitude. Gratitude allows you to dance with zest, love, and passion. It also allows you to sing with joy. Why?

No matter the dance step you are doing or the tempo, gratitude adds a sense of well-being and happiness to your life that comes from no other source. With gratitude, you can dance, love, and sing your way to create your own piece of heaven on earth. With more happiness and better relationships, your life will be a fulfilling dance!

Progress

In relationships, progress through positive energy, and your ability to bond comes when you accept change. The one constant in life is change. Therefore, you must change, even in long-term relationships, to adapt and to remain relevant.

Change requires giving up old patterns that you feel comfortable with, even if they are hindering you. However, change also requires that you embrace a new way that brings discomfort and, very often implicitly, brings difficulties.

Yet you, we, resist change. Why? We focus on what we have to give up instead of what we have to gain. When change comes to a relationship or anything in life, it will come about more quickly if you focus on what you have to gain. That is how you make progress.

Know Your Role

To have better and more positive relationships, you must know your role. Very often, this is a process. It is a voyage of discovery and takes time. Once you discover and understand your role in a relationship, then you have a decision to make. You can expand the relationship, or you can limit your exposure to it. Or you can terminate it and move on.

Become clear on your role. Understand it. You will make better decisions on the value your relationships bring you and what to do about them when you do.

Why Are You Climbing?

The reason you climb the mountains of life affects your relationships. Are you climbing the mountains so others will see you? Or are you climbing so you can see more of, discover more of, and be more to the world? When you climb so others will see you, they will applaud, appreciate your performance, and move on. Why? They can see it is all about you.

But when you climb to enlarge yourself as a person and make it evident that's your sole purpose, others will see that you are all about you. When you add value to yourself, it is an opportunity to add value to yourself and others. When people sense that they find it attractive. Adding value to others can act as a magnet to creating more positive, successful relationships.

Don't Get Hung by Your Tongue

Two major components of any successful relationship are the words you use and the tone with which they are delivered. For better relationships, focus on what you have to be grateful for. Express this gratitude in your words. Have positive intentionality. Be positive on purpose.

Look for the good things to talk about that can bring peace and even prosperity to a relationship. There is life and death in the power of your tongue.

In the Bible, Samson slew one-thousand Philistines with the jawbone of an ass. Yet, I have seen that weapon used every day on ourselves. Don't get hung by your tongue. Have positive intentionality. Respect the power of your tongue.

Fundamentals and Success in Relationships

What are the fundamentals of relationships? Two of the most important ones are attitude and character. You have control over them.

To have a good life, your legacy will be in the quality of your relationships. All of us must understand that we cannot be who we are without others. Be grateful for others.

When life ends, which it will for all of us, how you related to and benefitted others is remembered most. Success is neither magical nor mysterious. Success is being remembered well for what you brought to others with your attitude and character.

Is It Going to Make Any More Sense Tomorrow Than It Does Today?

Procrastination. I once had a mentor who asked me, "Is it going to make any more sense tomorrow than it does today to do what you need to do, the right thing?" Procrastination cultivates a lack of a sense of urgency in our minds. Without a sense of urgency, it is harder to get things accomplished.

Procrastination happens because we don't think something matters. It increases the odds of failure in our relationships, businesses, and lives. Why? No one likes to feel taken for granted. So have the attitude that says, "Do it today!"

Don't procrastinate. Have a sense of urgency! Value others and add value to your relationships.

Trust Is Your One-Way Road

Trust is your one-way road leading you to better relationships. Conversely, breaking trust takes you off the road to healthy relationships, never to return.

The People Around You

Surround yourself with people who see the greatness within you. Very often, we need the mirrors of other people to see the greatness within ourselves.

To be more certain of having the right people around you, ask yourself these questions about your relationships: How are they influencing my thoughts, actions, business, and life? Is the influence good or bad? Once you have the answers, they will guide you to create the pathways to accelerate the process of your successful performance.

Staying in the Game

We all face tremendous stress and adversity at times, which affects all areas of our lives, including our relationships. Stress can bring anger to the surface. Your anger is valid. It is what you choose to do with your anger that either keeps you in the game with your relationships or puts you on the sidelines.

When angry, whenever possible, turn your anger and energy toward something positive. You will create the opportunity to be happier. How? Ask yourself, what am I learning about myself that is showing me where I can improve?

Studies have shown that you will have an edge in your relationships when you bring positivity. This edge is not only about moving through stress and adversity. It also gives you better odds of keeping your relationships in a good place. That's staying in the game!

 **KEY TAKEAWAYS**

✓ Find the best in others, and they'll see the best in you.

✓ Harness your anger and turn it into something positive.

✓ Watch who you hang out with; surround yourself with people who influence you for the better

✓ Don't use words to hurt other people; pause and think before speaking.

✓ Let go of painful experiences and take one step at a time to move forward.

CHAPTER 9

The Power of Encouragement

TWO FROGS NAMED Will and Fern fell into a deep pit together. At first, they thought it would be easy to jump out. But after many failed attempts, they cried for help, and a crowd of animals gathered around the pit.

Everyone agreed it was hopeless. So, they urged Will and Fern to accept their fate. The harder the trapped frogs jumped, the more the crowd yelled at them to give up. Finally, Will stopped trying. Fern refused to quit, and with one mighty try, she leaped out of the pit.

The crowd was amazed. Someone asked Fern why she kept trying when everyone told her there was no chance.

Fern was baffled. "What are you saying?" she asked. "I'm a bit deaf. I was sure you were all cheering me on. I couldn't have done it without your encouragement."

This story highlights the importance of positivity and encouragement. In our relationships, we need to bring this to ourselves and others. You can help those you care about when they are down and out to get up and out.

All of us get into pits of our own making. But when enough people care, the possibilities of getting out of the pit increase. Show confidence in others. Encourage others. It will give them the confidence they need to keep trying and hopefully, eventually, with the extra strength from your encouragement, to jump out of the pit.

There will always be people in your life ready to tell you what you can't do. Real friends root for you, support you and help you discover your inner talents and strengths. This encouragement will enable you to reach further and jump higher.

Additional Observations from
The Relationship Zoo

Self-Talk Up or Self-Talk Down

What do you say when you talk to yourself? Are you receiving expert advice? Or are you going to embark on a fool's errand? Your self-talk is either putting you on the escalator going up, or the escalator headed down. You, and all of us, have expertise in both. Make sure your self-talk has you riding the escalator that is going up.

What you say with your self-talk will impact your business, life, and relationships. Remember, if you want to go up, you can't talk down.

Offering Help

You can't help everyone, but you can help someone. Unfortunately, offering your help to others can be like wading into a swamp. Suddenly, you are encountering snakes, alligators, and other dangerous situations. Relationally, things have deteriorated. It would be best if you got out.

For your help to have an impact, you must know your strengths and your weaknesses. Be clear about these. They will keep you from wading into the swamp of someone's problems. Be selective. When you are, you will be happier. Why? You will understand and apply yourself only to those people and situations where you and your strengths can have the greatest positive impact.

Optimism

Optimism is faith that you and your life can and will get better. Optimism is about hope and confidence. Hope and confidence springing from optimism make you feel good about yourself and your world. Optimism is critical to healthy, positive relationships and your well-being.

Your optimism is like a magnet in your relationships.

Your optimism is like a magnet in your relationships. It increases the odds of attracting people into your life who are optimistic and doers. All of us must have faith in ourselves to see achievement and better outcomes. What you see and manifest in yourself is what you will attract in your relationships.

Rudeness

Rudeness is low self-esteem trying to masquerade as strength. When someone has to talk over you, show contempt, constantly interrupt, and the list goes on and on, they are coming from a position of weakness. They cannot find strength within themselves.

These people do not feel good about who they are, and as a result, do not like themselves. They then project this dislike of themselves onto others, causing others to distance themselves from them. This behavior creates complicated, unrewarding relationships because others will only be with them because they *have* to, not because they *want* to.

Bounce

In your relationships, things are not always going to go well. Sometimes people, circumstances, or things are beyond your control. How you bounce when things are not going well will determine the path the relationship will take. Bounce is about coping skills. When things go wrong, how do you bounce? Setbacks, disappointments, and failures are the flip side of the coins of triumph, happiness, and success. Cope well! Live well! Bounce well! You will have better relationships.

If You Have to Tell Someone You Are Something

If you have to tell someone you are something, then you probably are not. Let your actions show people who and what you are.

Too often, we tell people what we are, the human "doing" and fail to show them who we are, the human "being." Only when they know the human being (who you are) will there be the trust to build relationships and explore opportunities with the human doing.

Show don't tell. That is the best way to be open to the possibilities of relating better to others.

The Time Value of Trust

The time value of trust is this: It can take days, weeks, months, or years to build. Trust can be broken in a second. And trust can take forever to repair.

Appreciation

Appreciation can change a minute, an hour, or a day. It can change a life. But for appreciation to affect the most significant change, you must be willing to put your appreciation of others into words. Only then, when it is clearly communicated, can others see it and feel it. And here's an extra plus when you express your appreciation with spoken words: Showing appreciation allows what is good in others to become part of you.

Time Flies

There is only one thing given to every human being equally and daily—time. Each one of us has the same amount of time in a day, 24 hours. And when we feel that we don't have enough time, we say that "time flies." But remember that when time flies, you are the pilot.

You are the pilot of your time, your life, and your relationships. As the pilot, you can spend more money. But you can't spend more time. Once the day is over, it is over. So be a good pilot and add value to yourself and others with the time you have. Adding value each day is the foundation for relationships that will take off and fly.

The Power of Your Thoughts

Thoughts are things that manifest themselves in how you speak, how you act, how you perform and how you show your emotions. In turn, these determine our relationships, results, and lifestyle. If we realized how powerful our thoughts are, we would keep our negative thoughts to a minimum. So how do you do this? For a better life, plant the seeds in your mind to acknowledge the good in every day. When you do, you will cultivate positive thoughts to propel yourself forward.

Relationships That Connect

Relationships that connect on a deeper level can mean the difference between prosperity and disaster. For example, during the coronavirus pandemic, I had a business owner contact me. He was afraid that his business would be declared non-essential and shut down as the restrictions became tighter. The definition of essential and non-essential businesses was general and could cause confusion.

He asked me who made those decisions about essential and non-essential businesses. The County Judge makes those decisions. I have a good relationship with the County Judge. I gave my friend his contact information.

After their communication, his business was determined to be essential, and the many people he employs continued to work. Being able to work was not only good for the employees but for the lives of the people who would have been negatively affected if they did not work. So, yes, relationships, sometimes just one relationship that connects on a deeper level, can mean the difference between prosperity and disaster.

Improve Your Relationship with Yourself

Holding on to what you cannot change is like wrestling with your shadow. It makes for a frustrating relationship with yourself. The shadow is visible, but you will be continually frustrated and unhappy because you cannot control or change it.

Some of the happiest moments in your life will come when you let go of wrestling with your shadows. Show the courage to let go. How do you do that?

Face the sunlight. When you do, you put the shadows behind you in the past, and you are now positioned to grow. And with your shadow behind you, you are set to improve your relationship with yourself.

How Are You Planning?

Are you planning your relationships around your life? Or are you planning your life around your relationships? At best, this can be a tricky balancing act. There isn't a right or wrong answer. Once again, the definition of balancing will vary with each person.

When you plan your life around your relationships, you are whittling yourself down by always taking care of others before you take care of yourself. Sometimes this must be done, and that is okay.

Long-term, a more positive way to live the life you want is to do what is best for you. Then plan your relationships around what is best for you. You may be accused of being selfish by not doing what someone else wants. When first used in the English language back in the Middle Ages, the word selfish meant self-preservation. When you preserve yourself, you have created the opportunity, a plan, to be happier. And when you are happier, you will increase the likelihood of having better relationships.

Commitment

Without commitment, you cannot have depth in anything, whether in learning, business, or your relationships. Commitment to your relationships will allow them to be deeper. Commit to first understanding the other person.

They will appreciate you discovering their values. They will feel you genuinely desire to get to know them as a human being. With a commitment to learning who people are, you are taking the first step not only *of* better relationships but relationships that will have depth and endure.

What Ripples Are You Creating?

Alone, you cannot change the world. But when you cast the stones of your character, thoughts, emotions, and influence across the vast pond of life, they create many ripples. And those ripples, your influence, may affect many people or a few.

There is one thing they will do for sure. They will dictate the nature of your relationships. All of us cast stones of influence. Are people and your relationships better for your influence? How are your stones being cast into the lives of others? What ripples are they creating? That is your legacy!

What You Believe About Yourself

What you believe about yourself is what you become. What you want to become without a belief in yourself will remain unattainable. What you believe about yourself puts the odds in your favor of it becoming a reality. What you achieve will define who you become. And who you become will determine the quality of your relationships and your life—the process to becoming more and having more starts with what you believe about yourself.

KEY TAKEAWAYS

✓ Remember that you are a human being, not a human doing.

✓ People want to know who you *are*, more than what you *do*.

✓ One simple relationship can make a difference between prosperity and disaster.

✓ Your influence has a ripple effect on other lives.

✓ Optimism attracts like a magnet.

CHAPTER 10

What to Compromise?

Issues versus Principles

IN SUCCESSFUL RELATIONSHIPS, compromise is a necessary ingredient. Of course, no two people are always going to agree. But hopefully, if you are in a close relationship, you share some of the same principles. Principles are truths that serve as the foundation for what you believe. Principles are points of view and beliefs where you are not willing to compromise.

Issues, on the other hand, are differences in points of view that can be compromised. For example, you and another person agree on the principle that eating lunch is a good thing. You each suggest a place to eat. Neither person likes the other person's choice. You continue your discussion and come up with a restaurant that is acceptable to both of you. You have compromised on the issue of where to eat while keeping the principle that lunch is good still intact.

The following story illustrates that if you compromise your principles in a relationship, your survival as a unique person could be at extreme risk.

The Story

It was a frigid winter day in Siberia when a hunter came upon a giant bear. The hunter was very cold and wanted the bear for his warm fur coat. As the hunter took aim and got ready to pull the trigger, the bear engaged him in conversation.

"Hey, wait a minute," said the bear. "You don't have to shoot me. Let's sit down and talk about this." As they talked, it became apparent what each needed.

The bear summed it up. "I am starving, and you need a fur coat. Let's see what we can work out."

So, the hunter and the bear talked some more. Finally, after a short discussion, a compromise was reached. The bear walked away with a full stomach, and the hunter was surrounded by a warm fur coat.

The hunter compromised the most important principle, doing what he must do to preserve his life.

To preserve yourself in your relationships, know each other's principles. Honor your principles. That is who you are. The only way to bring the best and authentic you into your relationships is to compromise issues and never principles.

Additional Observations from
The Relationship Zoo

Anger Is Acid

Anger is acid. In the chemical business, acid is stored in containers that are manufactured to hold it safely. With human beings, it is different. Anger is an acid that harms us more than any person we choose to pour it on when we store it. Yet, anger is a valid emotion.

As with emotions, how we hold and choose to do with them affects us and our relationships, positively or negatively. For example, holding onto intense anger will have unhappy consequences and negatively affect your relationships. Why? What is on the inside of you, the toxic acid of anger, sooner or later manifests itself on the outside.

And when it does, it may generate temporary compassion. Still, ultimately it eats away the positive bonds that are the necessary foundation for solid relationships.

Ability, Motivation, and Attitude

Ability is important. It gives you capability in certain areas, but it is not everything. Motivation, when added to ability, fuels the fire to use your ability. Yet, motivation by itself and even coupled with ability is not enough.

A "can do and will do" attitude is necessary for your ability and motivation to create the steam to drive your high-performance engine. When you apply an excellent attitude to your ability and motivation, you will move your business, life, and relationships from ordinary to extraordinary.

What Are You Giving?

Love yourself first. Only then can you give love to others. You can't give what you don't have. So, add a little chocolate, a little sweetness to your relationships every so often. It will be better for you and those who are a part of your life.

New Beginnings

New beginnings are very often hard to recognize because they come dressed in the clothes of painful endings. Without a finish, painful or not, there cannot be a new beginning. When something needs to conclude in your relationships or life, don't extend it and tolerate the pain. End it. You will create a new beginning and feel empowered for having taken action to improve your life.

Are You a Magnet?

If you aren't even drawn to yourself, who wants to be drawn to you? You must understand your *own* magnificence. You must love and respect yourself. Only when you love yourself, and the good that is in you can you constructively love others. You can't expect others to give you what you can't give yourself.

Loving and respecting yourself will function as a magnet to better relationships. You will project love and respect to others. And that's a large part of the formula for better relationships and happier life.

Alone Or Lonely?

Being alone is a choice. On the other hand, loneliness is either your choice or inability to connect well with others. Indeed, loneliness can happen because of circumstances. Most often, though, it is driven by your choices. Be careful of loneliness. It will cause you to make poor choices in many areas. And those choices are not conducive nor a foundation for good, solid relationships.

What Are You Learning from Others?

All of us have to have some learning to exist, let alone survive. We can learn from the books we read, the TV shows we watch, and social media, to name a few. But one of the most important sources of learning is your relationships with others. With others, the key is to make sure that you are not allowing what you learn from them to plant weeds in your mental and emotional garden.

What do you do when you, as all of us do, find a weed? You learn that you must pull it out by the roots. In your relationships, determine if people are planting weeds or creating beautiful flowers in your garden. If they are not making beautiful flowers, limit your exposure to these people and, even better, delete the relationship unless they are essential to your life.

Get in the Game

To live every day of your life, you must get in the game. Relationships are a contact sport. Nothing is accomplished while sitting in the stands or on the sidelines, where you are a spectator. Get on the field. When you do, you will demonstrate your value to yourself and others and start building relationships.

These relationships will move you from existing through life, on the sidelines, to experiencing life's potential and its rewards. This will happen because you have chosen to live every day of your life by getting in the game.

The Trust Account

Trust in relationships is like money in the bank drawing compound interest. For a bank account, you can make a withdrawal and still hold onto the account. But when you withdraw trust from your relationship account, it can quickly become overdrawn, bringing an end to the possibility for future healthy relationships.

Give Compassion to Yourself

Give compassion to yourself. When you do, you will open your heart. And when you open your heart, it will transform your life. How?

When you give compassion to yourself, only then can you gift compassion to others. Compassion not only affirms what others are experiencing, but it does something more substantial. It affirms who they are. And that affirmation, when properly placed, can positively transform your relationships and life.

...when you open your heart, it will transform your life.

Winning

Winning is not being the same person today as you were yesterday. You have decided to grow, learn, and develop. And to do these things daily. Your personal development will allow you to attract better relationships, leading to a happier and more fulfilling life. So consistently grow, learn, and develop. It will make you a winner every day!

Surfing

When you experience a wave of emotion, you have a choice. You can surf it, or you can let it pass. Just like a surfer chooses which waves to ride, you have the power to do the same with your emotions. Why is this important? Emotions drive logic, not the other way around.

Whatever you believe logically has an emotion attached to it. How you express your feelings and the degree to which you express them will dictate which waves you will choose to surf. Choose to ride the waves that are more likely to lead to greater connectedness and deeper relationships. Let the others pass by. It is your choice!

Who Is Pursuing You?

The skills and disciplines you develop will elevate you and bring value to determine who pursues you. Change it if you don't like who or what is seeking you or attracted to you.

Change means that you must grow in a different direction. Change requires you to move—change who and what you value. When you do, other people and opportunities will pursue you. You can make the change. You can move. You are not a tree!

Count Your Blessings

Count your blessings every day! Over weeks, months, and years you will come to appreciate how many days you have been blessed. It is astounding!

Ponder the good. Be grateful. And be appreciative. When you count your blessings, you will pass these along into your relationships and create opportunities for better and more positive connections.

Relationship Dynamics

I cannot be me without you. You cannot be you without me. Your reflections in the eyes of others define your relationships. There are certain things I cannot do that you can. There are things that you cannot do that I can. But, together, we can do so many more good things. Alone we can do so little. Together, in a positive relationship, we can do so much.

What Is Your Legacy?

What you do for yourself today is gone when you die. Yet, the things you do for others will be your legacy. They will be the things after you are gone that others will remember about you.

I was meeting with someone I have known for several years. One day I realized that I had never heard her talk about her mother, who died several years ago. So I asked her about her mother, and there was silence. Then she said, "All she cared about was herself and her activities."

It was a stark reminder that how you care for others and your relationships with them is how you will be remembered. So, what is the legacy you are building?

Commander In Chief

You are the Commander in Chief of your life. In your relationships, you can hire, fire, and promote individuals. Tied into those relationships are the circumstances and things we experience with others. All of us make mistakes.

It's not about being perfect. Knowing when to hire, fire, or promote and, most importantly, having a process for yourself on how to do them, will determine to a great extent your levels of happiness and satisfaction in your relationships and life. Be your Commander in Chief!

What Is Your Focus?

What is your focus in your relationships with others? If your focus is on the results you will get from changing others, your connections will be tenuous at best and full of unhappiness at worst.

For stronger relationships, focus on how you can change. Change does not mean changing your values, although that can be beneficial. Change means changing your attitude and approach to others. When you do, you will get better results. Better results in your relationships and life come from your focus on change, and most importantly, to be the change. Change yourself. This is the focus that can lead to better relationships.

Be On Speaking Terms with Happiness

To have happiness in your relationships, you must express and feel gratitude, not just for the relationship but for all the good things in your life. If you never learn how to express gratitude, you will never be on speaking terms with happiness. Gratitude tells about the things for which you are happy. Only with gratitude can you have happiness, which allows you to connect with others on a deeper level.

 **KEY TAKEAWAYS**

✓ Counting your blessing will probably surprise you!

✓ Open your heart of compassion to affirm others.

✓ Winning isn't as much about competition as it is about personal growth.

✓ You have the honor of hiring, firing, and promoting people in your life.

✓ Anger is a harmful poison in your life when not handled positively.

CHAPTER 11

What's Poking Its Nose into Your Relationships?

IN THE DESERT, one thing that the Bedouins (*the people who wander the desert from oasis to oasis*) always guard against at night is the camels trying to get into the tent. If left untethered, the camel will poke its nose a little bit under the edge of the tent and lift its head. Then it will do it again and lift up a little more. After a few times, now, the camel's head and neck are inside the tent. And, with little more effort, the camel now has uprooted the moorings of the tent, and it is now on top of him.

The camel is now in control. In our relationships, we have to be aware of our untethered camels. Untethered camels are relationships, where if we don't tether them by either limiting or eliminating their influence, they will take over and control our lives.

What are you letting poke its nose into the tent of your life?

What relationships and thought patterns and circumstances around your relationships are you letting poke too far to where it takes over like the camel?

Only when we take action to tether the camels and put them in a safe place can we lead our lives for ourselves and make the choices in priorities and relationships that lead to a better life.

Take a look right now at who is poking its nose under your tent. An excellent place to start is to look at who you are tolerating more than enjoying.

Additional Observations from
The Relationship Zoo

Hurt

None of us like to be hurt in our relationships. And when you are hurt, you can get stuck, which takes you down mentally and emotionally. Also, when you are hurting, you have questions for which there aren't good answers.

Why did this happen? I can't believe they did what they did. And there are many more. If you have been hurt in a relationship, you must change your thinking to take you out of the downward spiral.

Start focusing on the lesson or lessons you learned. That is the only way you will continue to grow. You must use your past as a school to learn from.

If you continue to focus on the pain, the hurt, you and your relationships will continue to suffer. This is because now you are using the past as a club on yourself.

Focus on what you have learned from the school of the past. Next time, what will you be aware of to avoid the hurt and get stuck on the pain and your unhappiness? Then, armed with your experience and what you have learned, you will start to move beyond the past and the hurt that will be better for you in your current and future relationships.

With and Without

With trust in your relationships, you have something. Without it, you have nothing.

The Downward Pull

What is the downward pull? It is a constant stream of negativity. It can come from many sources. One source is your relationships. How do you know if someone has become a downward pull, a bug, or a weed in your life? Ask yourself after you have been with someone: "Do I have more positive energy?" Suppose the answer, more often than not, is no. In that case, it is time to limit or delete the relationship that is stealing your energy. That is how you stop the downward pull.

Listen to be Understood

Communication will fall apart in any relationship when we do not listen to understand. Unfortunately, as we listen, we are often crafting a response that diverts our attention from what the other person is saying, how they are saying it, and the emotional inflection of the words.

Be fully interested in what the other person is saying. Once they know that they have influenced you to listen to them with exclusivity, only then will they be ready to listen and understand you. So be interested in others' communication. That will make you interesting and encourage others to listen on a deeper level to understand you better.

What Are You Chasing?

People notice what you are chasing. When you pursue the wrong things, people will find ways to avoid you. But interestingly, when they see you chasing the right things, they will find ways to catch you in a relationship.

Success and good relationships are not to be pursued. In that pursuit, you often reach for the wrong things that will make you feel better but that do not make you better. Success, the right things, and good people are attracted to you by the person you become. Pursue being a better person. You will attract the right things and better people. Only then are you positioned for improved relationships and greater success to find you.

Find Peace with Others

If relationships were a science, we would have a formula for every relational situation. We would follow the formula and have success. Unfortunately, relationships are not a science. They are an art form where you create the brush strokes. What works for one person may not work for another.

If you want to find peace in your relationships with others, you must first find your own internal peace. You can't give what you don't have. Instead, create peace within yourself with gratitude, kindness, care, and appreciation for others. Only then can you give peace to others.

Proof

When in a relationship, trusting someone is your decision. Proving you right is their choice.

Respect, Kindness, and Generosity

Respect, kindness, and generosity are three elements in good relationships. Where do they come from? They come from good self-esteem. Do what you can every day to feel good about yourself. It will boost your self-esteem. Only then can you give to others in your relationships what you would like to receive from them. What you can give, you are more likely to receive.

Relational Satisfaction

In looking at your life, you will begin to realize that your greatest satisfaction comes from the pleasure and good you brought to other people's lives. It is not when you prevailed or outdid someone. For greater relationship satisfaction, the best competition is to become a better version of yourself. Outdo yourself and defeat your fears. When you do, you will inspire and bring pleasure to others in your relationships because you have chosen a path not only for a good life but a life well-lived.

What Am I Accumulating?

Your relationships are the sum of your efforts repeated every day over some time. If those efforts are positive, very often, a more profound connection is established. You can say this is a successful relationship because, in many ways, it works for both of you. On the other hand, failure in relationships is the repetition of many minor errors in judgment repeated every day over a while.

Neither success nor failure is a single grand event. Success and failure are either the accumulation of good actions or ones that bring a negative response. As you go through your relationships, it is always good to check yourself by asking this question:

"What am I accumulating?"

Be...for Better Relationships

Be firm but not overbearing. Be kind but stand your ground. Be self-aware but not self-centered. Be appreciative of your gifts and talents but not arrogant. Aim for these character traits. Sometimes you will miss it. But keep targeting them. For your efforts, you will have a better business, life, and relationships.

Keep Perspective in Your Relationships

Very often, you can be misguided in your view of your importance in a relationship. You may be more important or less important to others than what you believe.

It reminds me of the relationships I have had with dogs and cats. My dogs generally worship me. My cats appreciate me at times but, for the most part, ignore me. I can't be the best for everyone. And everyone can't be the best for me. Keep this perspective. In your relationships, some people will be like dogs while others will be like cats. That's okay. Accept it, and you will have a more peaceful perspective that will be better for you and your relationships.

Be Grateful

Be grateful for your relationships. They define you. Without them, who would appreciate your gifts and your talents? And who would warn you when you are straying off course or into danger? So be grateful for your relationships. Whether positive or negative, they can teach you something that will improve your life and the lives of those you touch if you are open.

Foundation for Better Relationships

The greatest gift you can give to yourself and others is making progress on your personal development. So instead of saying to others, "I will be interested in doing something for you if you first do something for me," try this approach.

Strive each day to be the best me—to be the best for others.

Take the focus off the other person and what they can do for you. Instead, look first at yourself and how you can personally develop in what you can do for them. For example, how can you add value? Only then are they more likely to look at themselves and have a desire to figure out how they can care for you.

Now I say: "I will take care of myself, and I will be best for you. And if you take care of yourself, that will be the best for the other people in your life and for me."

The result: My goal is to strive each day to be the best me—to be the best for others. That is the foundation for good relationships.

Priceless to Useless

Once you have trust, it is priceless. Once you lose it, you are useless.

Long-Term Success

Long-term success in relationships comes from two actions. First, you must build credibility, trust. Trust is the foundation. To have loving and enduring relationships, there must be mutual trust.

The second action is the harder one for most people. Consciously choose who you are going to associate with. People who cannot be trusted or who are negative, to name a few, or who don't share your values must be severely limited or deleted from having access to you and your innermost thoughts. Sometimes this is not possible. But most of the time, you do have a choice. For greater long-term success in your relationships, choose those who share your values and who you can trust.

Someone Does Need to Meet You

Only when you can be yourself will others give you the feedback to let you know who you are. When you are clear and know who you are, you will learn to connect with others to add value to your relationships. Yes, someone does need to meet someone like you, but only if you know who you are on the inside and manifest it authentically on the outside.

Better Relationships with Others

What can you do to have better relationships with others? Be happier! Have a go-give attitude. Give kindness, and you are more likely to have kindness come back to you. Give appropriate support, and you will have the support of others. When you give what is good to others, you have created more possibilities for happiness in your relationships.

Past, Present, and Future Relationships

Past relationships are those that you had at one time but are no longer part of your present. Present relationships are the people you deal with today and regularly.

Yet, the most important relationships will be your future ones. So always be looking to form new, positive relationships. These relationships will have you climb mountains and see vistas that are unimaginable today.

But to see this beautiful future, you must let go of those relationships in the present that keep you from climbing to new summits. To do this, you must not dwell on the past and be proactive in the present about the future you desire. Poor past and present relationships will keep you anchored and unable to move forward.

The key to reaching new levels of success and happiness in life is to pack your backpack with the right supplies, people with good attitudes, and ultimately people who will encourage you to climb to the future you desire.

Attitude Is the Difference

In the big picture, there is little difference in what we experience. All of us go through life with its trials, tribulations, and rewards. Yet, there is one thing in each of us that makes a big difference, not only in how we view ourselves and our lives but in our relationships. It is our attitude about ourselves and others. Quite simply, with our attitude, we are either positive or negative. All of us can be hurt by the words and the actions of others. But, on the other hand, all of us have blessings bestowed upon us.

Your attitude about what hurts you and what blesses you will determine who comes into your life and the quality of your relationships. Attitude is the difference.

 **KEY TAKEAWAYS**

✓ Trust is a must when it comes to loving and enduring relationships.

✓ Be grateful for ALL of your relationships, not just the positive ones.

✓ Success and failure aren't just single, one-time events.

✓ Relationships with a downward pull rob you of energy.

✓ Be mindful daily of what you are pursuing or chasing.

CHAPTER 12

Improving the Quality of Your Life

DEVELOPING NEW disciplines and skills is one way to improve the quality of your life. But there is another way that will have an even greater impact than your disciplines and abilities. To improve the quality of your life, be a better you, and you do this through having better relationships.

The influence of others in our lives is enormous. Who are the people influencing your life? In the following story, it becomes abundantly clear that you can become something more than ever thought you would be with the right relationships. The right relationships allow us to become more than we ever could if we were alone.

Here's the story.

There is a museum in Paris, France, which has beautiful rose-colored marble floors. Once you enter the museum, standing at the front of the museum on the rose-colored marble tile floors is a beautifully sculpted rose-colored marble tile statue.

Hundreds of thousands of visitors visit the museum each year. And one of the main attractions of the museum is the rose-colored marble tile statue.

One night after the museum closed, the floor and the statue got into a conversation. The rose-colored marble tile floor was very troubled. He was angry.

He asked the statue: "Why is it that hundreds of thousands of people come to look at you while all they do is walk over and not notice me? How come? It is not right!"

The statue thought for a moment and replied.

"We both came from the same quarry. We are cut from the same stone. But I allowed others to touch me, shape, mold, and sculpt me into something better."

Then the statue added: "You did not allow others to bring their wisdom and influence to make you more than a slab of marble."

Let the right people into your life, and they will touch, shape, and mold you to be more than you ever could be by yourself.

Don't go it alone.

If you do, your life will be flat, like the rose-colored marble tile floor. And like the marble tile floor, your life will be about people not recognizing the good in you because you have chosen to keep it to yourself. So, like the floor, your beauty will not be visible.

Be like the statue. Let others touch, shape, and mold you to be something better. Only with the help of others can we have and experience the relationships that allow us to become more and attract more.

Additional Observations from The Relationship Zoo

Successful Relationships Are Built

Successful relationships are built on looking for opportunities to help others. Unsuccessful relationships are about "What's in it for me?" Are you a positive collaborator who offers support to others? Or are you a negative manipulator who seeks only to win for yourself? To have long-term success create win-win relationships. Win-lose never builds trust or collaboration. As a matter of fact, it isolates you from success. Success depends on "we" and not "me."

Applaud the Small Steps Forward

Too often, in relationships, you can pick on the small things that irritate you. Over time this constant negative picking can become a big thing. And, at times, it is justified. Here's the problem—your focus on the negative causes you not to applaud the small, positive steps forward.

A relationship, in many ways, is like a baby. We don't know how babies will act or why they act the way they do. But when babies take their first steps and fall, we applaud them. We encourage them. We don't criticize that they fell.

Instead, we celebrate that they tried. They tried to be better. So, in your relationships, applaud the small steps forward. This response will encourage more significant positive steps which can take you and your relationships to a happier place.

What Do You Think is Valuable?

What you think is valuable is the foundational connection in all your relationships. The more you and someone else agree on what is beneficial in terms of your values and how you choose to conduct your life, the greater the possibilities for a deeper relationship.

If you want more meaningful relationships, look at what you think is valuable. It starts with your philosophy. What's your philosophy? It is a direct reflection of what you think is worthwhile. What you feel is valuable determines your attitude, activity, and results. Therefore, it is of enormous importance.

As each day goes by, what are your choices saying about what you think is valuable? If what you think is valuable is working in your life and relationships, that is great. If it is not, change it. Embrace change in what you think is valuable. When you do, you will expand your life, and you will be open to opportunities for better relationships.

Emotional Links

Emotional links determine how you position yourself in a relationship. Some links are good. And some are not. The ones that are not are the ones that are hardest to break. Resentment of others is one of those negative emotional links. Resentment of others allows them to occupy rent-free space in your mind and heart.

All of us have resentments. But how do you resolve negative emotional links? Through forgiveness. The quicker you can forgive, the sooner you can get on to a better path to your fulfillment. The key benefit to forgiveness is it frees you, allowing more positive things to occupy the rent-free space in your mind and heart.

When To Exit

In relationships, there are various roles we play. These can be good. But if you find yourself playing the role of detective, it is time to exit the relationship.

For Better Relationships Improve the Process

No one likes to receive criticism. Criticism is necessary for improvement. But the challenge in criticism, in many cases, is in how it is delivered. And how it is delivered determines if the relationship is going to be closer or become more distant.

The criticism that is most effective looks first at improving the process. And it could be a process that is causing the problem, as opposed to the person. But, interestingly, very often, when the process improves, the person becomes better. They are inspired to do what is right and follow your leadership because your focus is on the process in the relationship. Why? Your focus was on *what* is right, the process, not *who* is right, the person.

Create Happiness in Your Relationships

Gratitude is foundational for happiness. In your relationships, bring gratitude. Gratitude is an attitude of feeling blessed. Understand and acknowledge what you are grateful for. Gratitude is about your blessings. And, when you focus on your blessings, it will create happiness inside of you that benefits you and your relationships with others.

Casualness

Casualness in how you handle your daily relational contacts can be deadly. The one off-handed remark, the attempt at humor insensitive to others, or the unneeded sarcastic remark, to name a few, all happen because you don't think it matters.

You become casual about them. Yet, it is these things that people end up remembering because they hurt or make them feel taken for granted that they use to define their relationship with you. Remember that everything matters. Casualness in your relationships can lead to casualties. And one of those casualties could be you!

Unplug

Suppose there is a problem with a computer, router, or another electrical device. In that case, the first step taken to restore functionality is to unplug the device. When it comes to our lives and relationships, the level of intensity can certainly cause distress.

Learn how to unplug. It will benefit your relationships...

129

Unplugging, when it comes to maintaining good relationships, is often tricky. Learn how to unplug. It will benefit your relationships because rest or taking a break allows you to be the best you can be for others.

Relationships That Connect

Lift others. Cheer one another on. You are not here to outshine other people or to get one up on someone. When you look up into the clear night sky, you see many stars. The world and your life would be pretty dark if you were the only star.

You are here to outshine your present self. In this growth process, you will give energy to others to where their stars will shine more brightly. When you lift others and cheer others on, you have a hand in creating many stars that brighten the sky of your life, thereby creating deeper connections and more meaningful relationships.

What Are You Touching?

When you want to touch the past, it is like touching a rock. It is not going to change. When you want to feel the present, you touch a flower or some other living organism. But if you're going to touch the future, then go and find someone's life you can feel in the present.

The past, like the rock, has no life unless you choose to give it one. Like the rock, you can't change the past. But, when you touch the present, you live in the moment and appreciate the life and people around you. When you feel the present, you can build a bridge to a better future for all. It positions you to touch the lives of other human beings positively.

When You Can Lose Value

There are no hard and fast rules when it comes to accessibility. In some of your relationships, you are readily accessible. You will return the phone call, email, or text as soon as possible. With other relationships, you will get back to them, but not with the same degree of urgency.

Look at your relationships. Are you too accessible? There is no hard guideline here. That is something you determine. But when you become too accessible, you will lose value.

First, it is hard to complete what you need to do with too many contacts from others because of the distractions. As a result, you can feel like you are falling behind. In your mind, you are not as valuable because you are not able to keep up. And in the eyes of others, you may not be as productive or responsible as you should be. In this case, it is crucial to set boundaries regarding what others should expect from you. Give others an expectation where it allows you to be more productive with less clutter in your day. Establish guidelines so you can be the best you!

The second way you lose value ties to the first. When you are readily accessible, others do not value you and your time. Not necessarily because of some malicious intent, but they do so anyway. As a result, they can take you and your time for granted, making you angry and resentful.

The degree of accessibility is different for each one of us. Regardless, look at your degree of accessibility. You lose value when you are too accessible.

The Biggest Comeback

All of us suffer disappointments in our relationships with others. And the resulting unhappiness is part of life. When these disappointments occur, how do you come back? How can you regain your happiness? One way is having the support of good people around you. But that alone is not enough.

To make a comeback, look at that past as a school to learn from. Ask yourself, what have I learned? Then, understand yourself on a deeper level as to what brings you true happiness and fulfillment. Doing this will create the pathways in your mind that you need to take to be happy.

After disappointment in your relationships, the biggest comeback is making yourself happy again.

Your Mental Health

Each of your relationships brings something to you. And you give something to them. Examine what someone in a relationship is bringing to you. Next, look at what you are giving to them. Suppose you are going through a great deal of mental and emotional gymnastics to justify a relationship. In that case, it is most likely best to move on.

Why? Relationships do things *for* us. But they also do something *to* us. There is a vast difference between "for" and "to." What they do to us shapes who we become as a person. Ask yourself: Is who I am becoming acceptable? If not, limit or delete the relationship. Stop sacrificing your mental and emotional health for other people.

What Are Others Bringing Out in You?

Do you wish for more happiness and fulfilling relationships? Honor yourself. Distance yourself from the people that bring out the person you are trying not to be anymore.

You Have Everything Going for You But—

You have intelligence, a good personality, good character. You are in a career that you love. Yet, you are unhappy. Your relationships are not that fulfilling. They end up coloring for better or worse everything else. It can happen to all of us.

What do you do? You have and are the total package, yet you don't feel it. Look at the people in your life. It is not about them being good or bad. It is about how they fit with you and your life. If they fit, maybe you can expand the relationship. If they don't, then possibly you need to limit or separate from them.

You are who you are. You are the total package with your gifts and talents. To whom are you delivering your gifts and talents? For a happier life, remember this: Change the address. You will find people who appreciate the total package that is you!

You are the total package, but you may be at the wrong address.

KEY TAKEAWAYS

✓ Positive mental health involves examining what your relationships are bringing to you.

✓ The biggest comebacks in life always involve learning from the past and acknowledging your disappointments.

✓ Being readily available to people at all times generally causes them to devalue you and your time.

✓ Sometimes you need to "unplug" a relationship to reboot it.

✓ To touch the future, be present in someone else.

CLOSING THOUGHTS FROM
THE RELATIONSHIP ZOO

THE POWER OF OUR WORDS in our relationships is enormous. The words you choose and how you use them are critical to successful relationships. Why? Words are our primary way of communicating with each other.

In writing this book, four themes kept coming to the forefront. And the words we use are integral to each one. And one of the four themes addresses words specifically. So what follows is a summary of each followed by a more in-depth look.

Most people in their relationships desire *happiness* and the peace and satisfaction that can come with it. Conversely, *bad moods*, poor attitudes, or negativity are undesirable and are the foundation for unhappy relationships.

Words. The words we use and the tone with which they are delivered have the most significant impact on our relationships. This is where we show the most consistency and are a primary indicator of our attitudes, beliefs, how we see ourselves and our world. The most significant number of wounds in relationships come from words.

Behavior. It can fall into two categories, contemplative and impulsive. Contemplative behavior is planned. Impulsive behavior is not. However, regardless of whether your behavior is contemplative or impulsive, you can make mistakes. At times, and with no ill intent, your behavior can be negative without you even realizing it. At this point, your words take over and either take what has happened toward more peace or turbulence.

Trust. Trust is essential to sustaining relationships. There will be great times in relationships; there will be hard times. There will be times that will tear us apart. But without trust, the glue that holds relationships together, we have nothing.

Happiness.

Everyone can bring you happiness. Some will do it by walking into your life. And some will do it by walking out. The easier part is bringing people into your life. The more challenging part, and where you can fail, is when you don't create an exit ramp for those who need to be out of your life. These are the people who need to be gone yet won't walk out.

You need to put these people on the exit ramp. And I wish I could tell you exactly how, but for everyone, it is different. So, for greater happiness, create your *own* exit ramp for those who do not fit with you and your values.

Bad mood. Bad words.

When you are in a bad mood, what are the words that you speak? Your mood can change, but the words you speak can never be replaced. The words you speak today are heard by the ears attached to the mouths that will repeat them tomorrow.

Choose your words wisely. Why? What stories do you want others to be telling about you? It is much easier to forgive or overlook someone's bad mood, let alone forget about it when bad words don't get in the way. For better relationships, be careful of the words you choose.

Bite your tongue or eat your words?

It is a choice you get to make in your relationships with others. But, to have more successful and fulfilling relationships in life, know when to bite your tongue. Yes, there are times to speak out. But knowing when to bite your tongue is critical to better relationships.

Biting your tongue is about tact. Tact is a choice. Tact is an emotional safety valve to let you maneuver from an uncomfortable situation without expending your mental and emotional capital. It gives you time to observe and to collect your thoughts. All of us make mistakes with words. Remember that when you have to eat the words you have spoken, you will constantly be reminded of them in the future, whether weeks, months, or years.

Behavior.

I had a behavior problem as a freshman in high school. I would talk in class while the teacher spoke, often costing me two hours of in-school detention. This meant sitting with others for two hours after school, doing absolutely nothing, while being supervised by a teacher.

I hated detention. When called out for my behavior, I would try to argue, using my words with the teacher to prevent getting another two hours of this boring punishment.

One day, the assistant principal sat me down and spoke words of wisdom that I still remember decades later. He told me, "Steve, you can't talk yourself out of problems you behave yourself into."

I did not learn the lesson right away. But over time, I got better. And I carried this wisdom into my relationships. It has helped me throughout my life. Words mean little if you do not change your behavior. Your words, when not supported by behavior, will make things worse. To change your relationships for the better, change your behavior. People will believe what they see. Your behavior tells others what you truly feel about them and your relationship with them.

As you go forward on your life's journey, my wish for you is that, in some way, this book contributes to happier and more fulfilling relationships.

Trust.

Without trust, the preceding categories do not matter. Trust is the most critical piece of the relationship puzzle. It is the foundation upon which everything else in a relationship is built. Trust is essential to build flourishing relationships, let alone ones that survive and thrive over time.

Trust is a daily undertaking that can take years to build yet break in an instant. And it can take forever, once broken, to repair. So, trust, or lack of it, exposes our fragileness as human beings.

When you have trust, it is the most incredible energizer and creator of forward-momentum in relationships. And when you don't have trust, it can stop a relationship from growing or destroy it. Trust can be like the wind— here one moment and gone the next, never to return.

For happier and more fulfilling relationships, become a keen observer of others. Can you trust them? Trust is an expensive present. Please don't give it to someone who doesn't appreciate such a valuable gift.

 **KEY TAKEAWAYS**

✓ Remember the four key building blocks in relationships:

✓ *Happiness* comes from both the people who enter your life and those who leave.

✓ *Words* guide the direction of your life. Choose them wisely.

✓ *Behavior* toward others is an outflow of your internal beliefs about yourself.

✓ *Trust* is a precious gift that you offer others. Without it, the relationship has nothing of value.

ABOUT THE AUTHOR

Rejection in relationships is the common thread that is the story that is Steve Scott's life. Yet, it was always rejection that forced or opened up opportunities for acceptance and new relationships. Some rejections were easy. Some were hard. And some were humorous.

After making it to the final 100 out of 3,000 plus applicants to audition for one of the last fifty spots in Ringling Brothers' Clown College, he failed to make it to be one of the final 50. At the time of his rejection, he was finishing his MBA at the University of Denver. Also, he was engaged to be married. However, that fell apart when his prospective father-in-law found out he wanted to be a clown.

He decided that the next most entertaining thing to do was land a real job in the business world. So, Steve went to work for a large national company, Levitz Furniture, and was transferred to Houston from Denver. That lasted about a year.

Steve's experiences in business and life have been entertaining and, at times, scary—from working undercover to successfully busting a pyramid marketing scheme. Then he bribed his way to the top of a military dictatorship in South America, to a run-in with military police, to being roughed up by former Nazis in Ecuador, to starting a service business that became the largest in the state of Texas.

All of these experiences happened and unfolded because of relationships. Since 2006 Steve has been a personal business coach and public speaker. In his business coaching practice, Steve's clients range from solo professionals to small business owners to large corporations. In all of these successful collaborations, relationships were the key to accelerating the process of successful performance.

In 2016 he published his first book, *Wings to Fly, Your Daily Lift Off to Soar to Greater Heights*, a daily reader to encourage and inspire greater performance, happiness, and success. In this current book, *The Relationship Zoo, Animal Stories, Human Insights: A Guide to Better Relationships*, Steve focuses on relationship observations and truths that can improve your life. He believes that success is getting what you want. And that happiness is wanting what you get. And without happiness, there is no true success. Happiness comes from having positive and enduring relationships.

His wish is that this book will encourage you and support you in building pathways to improved relationships and greater happiness.

WHAT OTHERS ARE SAYING

ABOUT THE RELATIONSHIP ZOO

You owe it to yourself to get lost in reading this book! It is an amazing read that immediately grabs your attention by comparing relatable animals to human intuition. Self-worth and self-care are critical factors to a healthy life. Steve allows you *to choose*—something that is a given right while meeting you where you are in your relationship journey, whether the relationship is good or needs improvement. He emphasizes words, behavior, and trust. Steve strategically allows the reader to start anywhere in the book to meet us where we are and give us control to have fun while learning. He lets you take a front-row seat into your own life and challenges you to decide what avenue works best for you while respectfully guiding you to an even more fulfilled and happier relationship with yourself and others.

While reading, I could not help but place myself in each situation and scenario offered. This book lets you examine yourself, your situations/relationships, strengths, and challenges comfortably while providing accomplishable solutions. Anyone who picks this book up, even for a quick glimpse through the pages, would benefit from it. So, what are you waiting for? Start making your life a more fulfilling and happier experience— read this book!

De'Andre J, Guin, Sr., *Drez Unlimited, LLC, Chief Operating Officer*

This book has no beginning or end, making it fun and free reading, delivered with personality and wisdom. Steve uses lessons to learn from the animals and applies them to life principles to enrich our lives and build better relationships. The key takeaways at the end of each chapter are helpful keys to having better relationships. But here is the best part. You can read as little or as much, at any time, in any order, and there will be something that you will come across that will enhance your everyday life.

Don R. Carpenter, Jr., *Retired, former Director of The Lone Star Convention Center*

Steve Scott's suggestion that "relationships are an art form and each of us puts our brush strokes on the canvas that is our relationships" presented me with clear insight into the authorship we each have in painting a Rembrandt for our life's relationships. Steve has done it again with thoughts that can improve your relationships every day. *The Relationship Zoo* is a fun, enlightening, and entertaining walk through the zoo of human nature and our relationships. Instead of cotton candy, I enjoy this book nightly with a glass of classy red wine. Cheers!

L. Jerry Bernhardt, *Author of Love Embers and Co-Owner of Bernhardt Winery*

Steve's timeless observations assisted me in discovering new views and ways of thinking. Most chapters begin with a tale about animals and their connections with humans that have direct parallels.

The story about Empowerment, Butterflies, and People highlights a lesson that we must encourage others to have good relationships. When we empower others, we allow them to struggle, learn, grow, and develop; empowerment provides the fuel through our love and assistance, enabling us to add value to themselves and create pathways to better relationships.

The story of the Frog and the Scorpion is the cornerstone of determining the right relationships. Most of us will encounter these questionable relationships when we are not sure of someone's character. Steve's story perfectly illustrates how being able to discern character can keep us out of harm's way. We must realize that even if someone is likable, we cannot fix a person's character. Instead, we must find out who *is* and who *is not* the "right" fit.

Another story centered around "The Power of Encouragement" and two frogs named Will and Fern. In our relationships, we cannot underestimate the importance of bringing optimism and encouragement. Optimism and encouragement are necessary to assist and support the people you care about to find a way to move forward when they are down and out.

Steve Scott is a seasoned master storyteller. This book is a daily must-read. Insightful and inspirational—it will help you improve and sustain better relationships, leading to greater peace of mind and happiness.

Greg Adams, *Frictionless Income Streams*

The Relationship Zoo delves into many relational issues to which we don't often give much thought. Clearly and concisely, Steve uses stories to highlight how a person can change the course of a relationship with thoughts and attitudes. This format allows the reader to easily read a passage that may change the trajectory of their day, week, or even life. It's a fun read and a recipe book for improving relationships, starting with the relationship one has with themselves, in a light and thoughtful package.

Kristi Adams

Steve Scott offers easy-to-relate insights into improving your relationships. This book is essential for every relationship in your life, whether it be your significant other, friend, or business acquaintance. I often found myself saying, "that's a situation I'm in" or "that's something I need to evaluate."

The stories and analogies were delightful and tied together with the concepts in each chapter. The ideas presented in each chapter create a foundation that will guide you toward deeper and more fulfilling relationships.

Dr. Lindsey Thomas, *Chiropractor with Sandstone Chiropractic Magnolia*

Relationships and the journey of self-improvement are fundamental in the fabric of one's life and often exemplify success or failure. Steve Scott eloquently paints the picture of how to create the most out of your relationships while revealing the invisible pits one call fall into when one is not conscious of the delicate balance. This book comes from the unique perspective of how animals behave in their natural habit and how humans often imitate similar patterns. Thus, it gives the insight to assimilate valuable relational tools in real-life relationships easily.

Nicole Preston. *General Manager of Community Impact Newspaper*

The Relationship Zoo is an easy read with a delineated takeaway for each chapter. As I was ideating over the concepts, it became abundantly clear that this book was about more than improving relationships with others. This book was a journey for developing a deeper self-insight.

The metaphors and narratives felt like either a lightbulb in my brain was just illuminated, or a bridge was formed that connected previous ideas I harbored before reading this book. As a Licensed Professional Counselor, I believe the words in *The Relationship Zoo* simply bring my work to life!

One of my favorite narratives was how poignantly Steve Scott captured the concept of positive thinking and attitudes with the dogs in the mirrors. This book is the perfect cocktail of philosophical insight and therapeutic highlights. It explains why it's essential to do what is right (rather than being right).

Rebecca Smith, MA, LPC-S, *Owner, Counseling Center of Montgomery County, Owner, Allied Co-Parenting & Family Academy, Founder, Love Heals You*

Steve has captured basic principles used in any personal or professional situation through stories that can relate to anyone. His animal stories and tales allow us to look at things from a different perspective and make them easier to remember. From the unconditional love we receive from a pet to unruly "indoor" and "outdoor" situations related to our *own* zoo of life, Steve helps us realize we need to talk less and listen more, and when we do speak, make sure we understand our message, audience, how it will come out, and how it could be perceived.

The Relationship Zoo heightened my awareness and understanding that there is no relationship without sincere trust. What are we even living for without them?

Scott Harper, *President, Conroe/Lake Conroe Chamber of Commerce*

Made in the USA
Columbia, SC
03 December 2021

50035836R00080